ECONOMICS
AND AMERICAN
EDUCATION

ECONOMICS
AND AMERICAN
EDUCATION

A Historical and Critical Overview of the Impact of
Economic Theories on Schooling in the United States

ALAN J. DEYOUNG

University of Kentucky

Longman

New York & London

Economics and American Education: A Historical and Critical Overview of the Impact of Economic Theories on Schooling in the United States

Longman Inc., 95 Church Street, White Plains, N.Y. 10601

Associated companies:
Longman Group Ltd., London
Longman Cheshire Pty., Melbourne
Longman Paul Pty., Auckland
Copp Clark Pitman, Toronto
Pitman Publishing Inc., New York

Executive editor: Naomi Silverman
Production editor: Ann P. Kearns
Text art: Hal Keith
Production supervisor: Kathleen Ryan
Cover illustration courtesy of the New York Public Library

Library of Congress Cataloging-in-Publication Data
DeYoung, Alan J.
    Economics and American education.
    Bibliography: p.
    Includes index.
    1. Education—Economic aspects—United States.
2. Public schools—United States. 3. Industry and education—United States. I. Title.
LC66.D49 1989   370'.973   88-26599
ISBN 0-8013-0064-9

89 90 91 92 93 94 9 8 7 6 5 4 3 2 1

This book is dedicated to my mother, Lynne DeYoung, and to my father, Dan DeYoung. Their encouragement and efforts on my behalf have been central in helping me to be in a place and time where this work could be written. It is also dedicated to my wife, Patricia. Her day-to-day efforts to help facilitate this final product were invaluable.

Contents

C

C

Foreword

Understanding the economic goals of schooling is essential for any student of American education. Alan DeYoung's *Economics and American Education* provides a clear and concise introduction to the economic thinking that currently dominates American education. Certainly by the 1980s and into the 1990s, concern with schools' educating future workers and aiding in economic development has displaced traditional goals of educating a democratic citizenry. As DeYoung argues, the linking of economic goals to schooling began in the early nineteenth century and had a major effect on school organization by the 1890s and the early part of the twentieth century. Through the rest of the twentieth century, economic arguments about children as human resources and the necessity of human capital development overwhelmed other goals for American schools. Currently, most school reform is discussed in the language of education's aiding in the competition for international trade and solving problems of unemployment.

The focus of DeYoung's text is on the arguments that were used to justify the use of schools for economic purposes. Beginning with economists like Adam Smith and Karl Marx in the nineteenth century, he introduces the reader to the linkages economic theorists made between education and the workings of the economic system. The last three chapters of the book are devoted to a critique of current economic goals for American schools. This book is a valuable introduction to the impact of economic theory on schooling for beginning and advanced students of education.

JOEL SPRING

Preface

Kentucky, the state in which I live and work, has historically been poor and the educational status of our schools has historically ranked "below average." According to our local newspapers and to important business leaders, there must be some connection. And in Kentucky and its surrounding states, school reforms believed consistent with the economic development needs of the region are widely touted and have been put into place. Of course, the attempt to "improve" education in the hope of providing for increased economic development is not merely a regional crusade here in the Southeastern United States. It has also become by now a well-rehearsed theme in the national media, in state and federal legislatures, and in the executive branch of our government.

To be frank, my own experience and my own research indicates that the relationship between education and economic development is much more complicated than the current wave of school reformers would suggest. For example, the Appalachian region of Kentucky, West Virginia, Tennessee, and Virginia (where I do my work) has for decades educated and then exported many of its children to the industrial centers of the Midwest and Northeast. In other words, while the abilities and skills of many of my region's young people have been well developed, much of its economic base has deteriorated rather than improved.

Given this seeming contradiction, and noting that no introductory text specifically about education for economic development (as it is currently championed) exists, I decided to write this book. Drawing on a host of writings in political economy, economics, sociology, history, and educational history, I have indeed found many interesting and competing interpretations about the relationship between education and economic development. On the other hand, I have also found that studies/observations/perspectives not in accord with the "ideology" of education for economic development tend to be either completely ignored or deemed of little consequence in many school reform agendas of the late twentieth century. This book attempts to trace the logic of economic development in the West, and specifically how such notions have influenced the evolution of public schooling in America. As well, a central concern of this work is discussing how our current school reform agenda in this country is directed at "improving" our schools by more effectively tying the nation's economic development interests to specific schooling outcomes.

I make no claims that this work provides compelling new perspectives on the relationship between education and economic development, or that it eloquently provides alternative visions about what the purpose of education ought to be. Rather, what I have set out to do here is to review what many, many others have written on this topic, and to briefly outline these arguments as made by far more talented individuals than myself. Rather than providing *the* answer on what is or what ought to be the relationship between education and economic development, I have attempted to underscore existing debates on this matter—I hope with some success.

ACKNOWLEDGMENTS

Most of this work draws from several disciplines and touches on a variety of academic themes. It therefore falls outside of any particular school of thought within the social sciences and/or the social foundations of education. Given the comparatively eclectic nature of this undertaking, then, there are relatively few of my colleagues who can take either the blame or the credit for what I have tried to write here. This is not to suggest that a variety of people have not attempted to keep me "on course" throughout my writing. Early suggestions for what I might include came from several international contacts, including Ross Harrold and Colin Lankshear. Here at home, Beth Goldstein and Dick La Brecque both supplied reading materials I found quite useful for certain chapters of this book. In addition, Dr. Brad Mitchell, of Ohio State University, and Dr. Henry Levin, of Stanford University, provided helpful comments on an early draft of this work. And finally, Flo Estes helped keep track of the chaos in my office and work. And finally, Flo Estes helped keep track of the chaos in my office and of the whereabouts of the manuscript, as a variety of projects have occupied my/our time during the past year.

Writing a book, of course, takes a lot of time and throws other domestic and teaching duties out of kilter. I would like to thank my wife for tolerating the writing schedule I tried to keep to during the course of this work. I'd also like to thank my chairman, Richard Angelo, for minimizing where possible the teaching and committee assignments I ordinarily deal with, and for the encouragement he gave me throughout this project. I want to thank Joel Spring for his insightful comments and suggestions from the inception of this project up through the final draft. And finally, Naomi Silverman at Longman Publishing deserves much of the credit for bringing this book to completion. I am sure she had (if she doesn't still) second thoughts about whether this project would ever come to be realized.

CHAPTER 1

Introduction

History is not kind to idlers. The time is long past when America's destiny was assured simply by an abundance of natural resources and inexhaustible human enthusiasm, and by our relative isolation from the malignant problems of older civilizations. The world is indeed one global village. We live among determined, well-educated, and strongly motivated competitors. We compete with them for international standing and markets, not only with products but also with ideas of our laboratories and neighborhood workshops. America's position in the world may once have been reasonably secure with only a few exceptionally well-trained men and women. It is no longer. . . . Knowledge, learning, information, and skilled intelligence are the new raw materials of international commerce and are today spreading throughout the world as vigorously as miracle drugs, synthetic fertilizers, and blue jeans did earlier. If only to keep and improve on the slim competitive edge we still retain in world markets, we must dedicate ourselves to the reform of our educational system for the benefit of all—old and young alike, affluent and poor, majority and minority. Learning is the indispensible investment required for success in the "information age" we are entering.[1]

This quotation from the 1983 National Commission on Excellence in Education captures the spirit of the educational reform movement that has been sweeping the United States since the mid-1980s. The message from this group and many others is loud and clear: American schools must alter both their goals and processes in the education of our children. Successful schooling in the United States, the Commission argues, must be better directed at turning out a workforce with the scientific and technological brain power to revitalize our stagnant national economy.

During the late 1970s and early 1980s, the United States fell behind and/or lost its competitive edge in the race for dominance of many world markets. American business leaders and policy makers, concerned that U.S.-made products were no longer internationally competitive, began to look for reasons why our market shares had fallen. Believing that the technological prowess of the American workforce is an important component of economic productivity, a number of concerned business leaders became interested in examining the content and direction of our public educational system. What they found, however, did not please them, particularly the declining SAT scores of the late 1970s and the mediocre performance of our high school students on international achievement tests.

Furthermore, at just the same time when it looked like our students were academically in decline, the educational achievement levels of students in economically advancing nations (like Japan) appeared much higher. Not surprisingly, many business leaders and politicians began to equate these two trends and to criticize American public schools for their role in contributing to a "rising tide of mediocrity." Such leaders have provided the major voice in current calls for school reform, particularly reforms that they see as beneficial to increased American economic development.

The 1983 National Commission on Excellence in Education report was but the first of a flood of documents issued by governmental and citizen task forces urging educational reforms designed to make the United States more competitive in international business circles (see Box 1.1). Another report released in 1986 by the Carnegie Forum on Education and the Economy makes a similiar argument:

> America's ability to compete in world markets is eroding. The productivity growth of our competitors outdistances our own. The capacity of our economy to provide a high standard of living for all our people is in doubt. As jobs requiring little skill are automated or go offshore, and demand increases for the highly skilled, the pool of educated and skilled people grows smaller and the backwater of the unemployable rises. Large numbers of American children are in limbo—ignorant of the past and unprepared for the future. Many are dropping out—not just out of school but out of productive society. . . . As in past economic and social crises, Americans turn to education. They rightly demand an improved supply of young people with the knowledge, the spirit, the stamina and the skills to make the nation once again fully competitive—in industry, in commerce, in social justice and progress, and, not least, in the ideas that safeguard a free society.[2]

Many in the education profession have also joined the school reform bandwagon and begun to reorient their notions about the purposes and processes of public schooling. For example, the National Education Association issued a report of its own in 1983 stating:

The critical link that exists between education and economic growth is at the heart of much of the current concern about the future of public education in our country. . . . A well educated citizenry and appropriately skilled labor force are essential to economic progress. Recent studies provide convincing evidence that past increases in U.S. productivity are attributable largely to educational gains and that shortages of skilled labor pose the greatest obstacle to future growth. . . . America faces an enormous challenge in restoring its economic growth. As we seek ways to meet this challenge, education must be a priority. It is, as always, the best investment in our people, which remains our nation's greatest resource.[3]

IMPLICATIONS OF CONTEMPORARY SCHOOL REFORM

Contemporary school reform advocates are primarily interested in educational changes that will theoretically lead to greater economic productivity in the United States. That is, both civic and business leaders at the end of the twentieth century have increasingly come to believe that sustained economic growth in the United States is essential to national progress and to view children as resources to be utilized in economic development. According to such logic, the mission and purpose of public education must increasingly be given over to developing such human resources. To the extent that the rest of us are also willing to so redefine the mission and structures of public schooling, it is clear that the emerging belief in education for economic development will have long-term, real, and profound effects on American educational policy.

Importantly, state and federal educational policies following from convictions that children are economic resources has and will continue to have dramatic impact upon the day-to-day lives of students and teachers in America's classrooms and schools. Many increasingly popular models for how to make schools "excellent" in the United States have often been guided by research into the school characteristics of those nations (like Japan) whose economic productivity has cut into American markets. Calls for increasing numbers of instructional hours during the school day, stiffening the requirements for teacher certification, beefing up the academic requirements in the secondary school curriculum, and collecting and publicly releasing achievement test score results, are all being accomplished around the nation under the guise that schools need to be tougher and more academically oriented than they have been in the past.

The media is also abuzz with reports of programs and reforms specifically linking the private sector with education in the United States (see Box 1.2). In an effort to convince the public and those running the schools that the needs of business and industry are synonymous with those of the school,

BOX 1.1   Reports on U.S. Reform

Reports on U.S. Reform Since "A Nation at Risk"

Following is a list of major reports on educational reform in the United States that have been published since the report of the National Commission on Excellence in Education, released five years ago this week.

1983

A *Nation at Risk,* National Commission on Excellence in Education, April 1983

"Report of the Task Force on Federal Elementary and Secondary Education Policy," Twentieth Century Fund, May 1983

"Academic Preparation for College: What Students Need to Know and Be Able To Do," The College Board, May 1983

"America's Competitive Challenge: The Need for A National Response," Business-Higher Education Forum, May 1983

"Action for Excellence: A Comprehensive Plan To Improve Our Nation's Schools," Task Force on Education for Economic Growth of the Education Commission of the States, June 1983

"Educating Americans for the 21st Century," National Science Board's Commission on Precollege Education in Mathematics, Science, and Technology, September 1983

High School: A Report on Secondary Education in America, Ernest L. Boyer, Carnegie Foundation for the Advancement of Teaching, 1983

1984

A Place Called School: Prospects for the Future, John I. Goodlad, 1984

Horace's Compromise: The Dilemma of the American High School, Theodore R. Sizer, 1984

"High Schools and the Changing Workplace: The Employer's View," National Academy of Sciences, May 1984

"Beyond the Commission Reports: The Coming Crisis in Teaching," RAND Corporation, August 1984

"Changed Lives: The Effects of the Perry Preschool Program on Youths Through Age 19," High/Scope Educational Research Foundation, September 1984

"The Unfinished Agenda: The Role of Vocational Education in the High School," National Commission on Secondary Vocational Education, November 1984

"Make Something Happen: Hispanics and Urban High School Reform," National Commission on Secondary Schooling for Hispanics, November 1984

1985

"Barriers to Excellence: Our Children at Risk," National Coalition of Advocates for Students, January 1985

"The Shopping Mall High School," Arthur C. Powell et al., 1985

"A Call for Change in Teacher Education," National Commission for Excellence in Teacher Education, March 1985

"Becoming a Nation of Readers," National Academy of Education, May 1985

"The Governors' Report on U.S. Education: 1991," National Governors' Association, August 1985

"Reconnecting Youth: The Next Stage of Reform," Business Advisory Commission of Education Commission of the States, October 1985

"Investing in Our Children," Committee for Economic Development, September 1985

1986

The Last Little Citadel, Robert Hampel, March 1986

"Tomorrow's Teachers," Holmes Group, April 1986

"A Nation Prepared: Teachers for the 21st Century," Carnegie Task Force on Teaching as A Profession, May 1986

"First Lessons," U.S. Education Department, September 1986

"Time for Results," National Governors' Association, September 1986

"School Boards: Strengthening Grass Roots Leadership," Institute for Educational Leadership, November 1986

1987

"Dropouts in America: Enough is Known for Action," Andrew Hahn et al., Institute for Educational Leadership, March 1987

"Public and Private High Schools: The Impact of Communities," James S. Coleman and Thomas Hoffer, April 1987

"Bringing Down the Barriers," National Governors' Association, August 1987

"Children in Need," Committee for Economic Development, September 1987

"James Madison High School: A Curriculum for American Students," William J. Bennett, December 1987.

1988

"New Voices: Immigrant Students in U.S. Public Schools," National Coalition of Advocates for Students, April 1988

Credits: "The Unfinished Agenda" series is being supported by a grant from the Exxon Education Foundation. (Reprinted with permission from Education Week, *Vol. 7, No. 31, April 27, 1988.)*

school–business partnerships have grown dramatically during the past five years. In addition, career days have become prominent features of public school life during the 1980s (and are even to be seen now in elementary schools across the land), as have invitations to local and state business leaders to attend public education forums, school board meetings, and

---

BOX 1.2   One Policy Initiative to Force Students to Stay in School

Business Group Reinforces Message to Georgia Students: Stay in School

A group of nearly 300 businesses around Dalton, Ga., have formed the "Stay in School" task force to help fight the high dropout rate by discouraging teen-agers from applying for full-time jobs.

City schools, and those in the surrounding Whitfield County, had a dropout rate of nearly 50 percent, according to C. Sue Phelps, assistant superintendent for the Dalton schools. Jobs in the local carpet industry often tempt teen-agers out of school.

In 1982, local businesses agreed to "discourage" teen-age non-graduates from applying for full-time work. Part-time employees still in school are sometimes required to keep up their grades or they will lose their job, Ms. Phelps said.

In 1987, Dalton schools reported a 12 percent decrease in the dropout rate. In Whitfield County the rate dropped 10 percent.

(Reprinted with permission from Education Week, *Vol. 7, No. 28, April 6, 1988.)*

BOX 1.3   Better Linking of the School with the Private Sector

Business Urged to Ask for Results

By Reagan Walker

WASHINGTON—Enlarging on his theme of accountability in education, Secretary of Education William J. Bennett said at a conference here that private-sector leaders who help build business-education partnerships should demand results for their contributions.

"When a business invests money in school programs, it should expect to see results in the way of better attendance, higher test scores, and fewer dropouts," Mr. Bennett last month told a group of 800 business executives and educators at the Fourth National Symposium on Partnerships in Education.

Pointing to what he called a substantial record of commitment—the formation by local and national businesses of partnerships with more than half of the nation's schools—Mr. Bennett said the business community now has a right to ask for a return on its investment.

"With the generosity, concern, interest, time, and investment that you put into partnerships, I hope you won't be reluctant to ask for results," he said.

The nation's 50,000 school partnerships range from programs that involve tutoring and career education to those that stress substance-abuse and dropout prevention, literacy initiatives, and postsecondary financial aid.

Mr. Bennett said that to aid the coordinators of such programs, the Education Department would publish another in its series of "what works" publications within a year, focusing on successful approaches to educational partnerships.

In predicting the future paths partnerships would take, members of a symposium panel said that one trend would be programs that could produce specific, measurable outcomes. They indicated that a major problem with current partnership efforts is their lack of focus.

Willie W. Herenton, superintendent of schools in Memphis, said partnerships would increasingly concentrate on early-childhood education, parent education, and job training.

He added that, to compel results, the business community would move toward programs that hinge on performance-based incentive grants for individual schools.

Mr. Herenton also stressed that partnerships should become more inclusive—involving government, the private sector, community-based organizations, and schools.

State initiatives, particularly matching-grant programs, are one of the best vehicles for fostering more inclusive partnerships, said Laurey Stryker, assistant commissioner of education in Florida.

She described the Private Sector and Education Partnership Act, passed by the Florida legislature this year, which appropriated $800,000 for strengthening partnership programs in the state and establishing the Florida Compact.

Florida is one of the first states to attempt a statewide program modeled after the Boston Compact, a nationally recognized education-business partnership in that city.

Gordon Ambach, executive director of the Council of Chief State School Officers, seconded Mr. Herenton's prediction of increased interest in early-childhood-development programs, but also noted two other areas likely to stimulate partnership efforts: the dropout problem and the changing nature of the U.S. workplace.

"The teaching profession is looking at empowerment and the quality of the work environment at the same time many businesses are looking at the exact same issues," Mr. Ambach said. "The two groups should share experiences and directly participate in the changes of the workplace."

Picking up Mr. Ambach's theme, Donna Oliver, the 1987 Teacher of the Year, urged business leaders to visit local schools to "observe the problems of the physical environment and get a sense of the demands on teachers' time."

In a speech that drew a standing ovation, she said business leaders should also use their political leverage to help candidates who support funding for public education.

The symposium was sponsored by the Presidential Board of Advisors on Private Sector Initiatives.

(*Reprinted with permission from* Education Week, *Vol. 7, No. 13, December 2, 1987.*)

PTO events—where they can take the floor to urge school leaders to better prepare future generations of American workers (see Box 1.3).

Good examples of the current campaign to link the needs of business with the outcomes of schooling can be seen in the efforts of two large national firms to "improve" schooling. Ashland Oil, for example, dedicated its entire multi-million dollar advertising budget in 1987 to a media campaign for reducing high school dropout rates and improving the quality of classroom teachers in the states of Ohio, West Virginia and Kentucky. Most of the ad campaign as it developed argued that the future of economic development in these states, and the quality of future workers coming to Ashland Oil, demanded significant reforms in school programs within these states.

Perhaps more ambitiously, the chairman of the Xerox Corporation went public with an official letter he sent to all of the candidates for the 1988 presidential election. In this letter, he likened the school's ability to supply adequately trained workers to the process that Xerox uses in obtaining other components for its industrial activities. In industry, if suppliers consistently turn out inferior parts, companies are free to seek new firms that can better meet their needs. The major problem with our schools, argued the Xerox chairman, is that they are poor suppliers of the manpower his company needs, yet they are the only "company" supplying laborers for our nation's industries. Thus, they need to be completely restructured.

> Despite its interest in education, the business community has been disappointingly unspecific about education reform. All of us who have been critics of public education, like myself, can no longer enjoy the luxury of criticism without accepting responsibility for suggesting ways to change the system. Our stake is too big. American business can expect to spend $25 billion a year in remedial training programs for new employees. Public education has put us at a competitive disadvantage—our workforce doesn't have the skills an information-based economy needs. Business and education have largely failed in their efforts to improve schools, because education set the agenda. The new agenda for school reform will be driven by competition and market discipline, unfamiliar ground for educators. Business will have to set the new agenda, and the objective should be clear from the outset: a complete restructure.[4]

BEYOND THE CONTEMPORARY SCHOOL REFORM REPORTS: AN OUTLINE OF THIS BOOK

This book is about the current generation of school reform proposals as they relate to the theme of education for economic development, and how our schools might better align themselves with such objectives. However, the analysis is much broader than this, for I seek also to explain historical precedents and trends in such thinking. And most importantly, I will attempt to lay out both the historical and contemporary criticisms of previous and current policy initiatives in the United States that would have schools conform to the ostensible needs of the private sector.

I undertake this task for at least two reasons. One of these (touched on in the preface) is that the political and popular rhetoric, suggesting that more education means more productivity for our economy, seems seriously misguided. And since the argument over the relationship between schooling and economic development has a long and interesting academic history, I believe an introductory text on this subject is long overdue.

However, analyzing the current call for school reform in the name of economic development is more than just an academic exercise. Contrary to what many teachers and teacher educators would like to think, I believe that political and economic trends in the private sector are frequently the primary determinants of pedagogical relationships in the classroom. As the several school reform policies illustrate, real changes in the nature of schools and the lives of those who operate them are occurring as a response to current calls for educational reform. While the particular strategies and proposals for school "improvement" now unfolding in American education may seem to some desirable and/or inevitable, it is important to understand the underlying logic that has brought them about. And, since there are important criticisms of proposals attempting to better relate the needs of the private sector to the purposes of schooling, such criticisms need to be understood by practitioners as well as by academics.

As stated earlier, current interest in using American public schools for purposes of economic development has a history of over one hundred years. However, the notion that a country's economic development is dependent on the abilities and acquired skills of its populace has an even longer history. Thus, the plan for this book is to trace historically some of the major concerns of economics as a discipline, paying particular attention to changing conceptualizations of the utility of public schooling as viewed by economists, social scientists, and policy makers. Given this emphasis, the chapters of this text are arranged chronologically. Chapter 2 begins by outlining perspectives of economic development and education first advanced by classical economists in the late eighteenth and early nineteenth centuries. In Chapter 3, the early history of education in the United States is presented, with particular attention paid to how arguments about education for economic development were cast, and to the centrality of such arguments in helping to form the American public school system. Then, as now, there were important competing theories about what education in America ought to look like, and about whether the public school had any place in the training of future American workers.

Chapter 4 explores the emergence of scientific methodology and the notion of social progress, particularly as economists and social scientists of the late nineteenth and early twentieth centuries used these concepts to discuss economic development. Chapter 5 focuses more specifically on how early twentieth-century school reform was informed by growing numbers of educational psychologists and educational sociologists, as they became interested in applying their perspectives to the causes of social progress and economic development.

Chapter 6 concentrates on contemporary research, theory, and practice relating economic development with the mission of public education. Of special interest in this chapter are the formalized concepts of "human capital" and "modernization theory," as these two economic and social science perspectives are now utilized to guide many educational policy decisions both domestically and around the world. Chapter 7 gives an overview of specific proposals for American school reform designed to aid the process of American economic development.

In the last three chapters of this text a variety of contemporary criticisms of current school reforms designed to improve the American economy and the economic fate of individuals is presented. Chapter 8 reviews a number of theoretical and methodological critiques of human capital and modernization theories as offered by various mainstream economists and social scientists. In Chapter 9, on the other hand, important "radical" critiques of both human capital theory and contemporary school reform are discussed. In addition, several perspectives critical of mainstream economic development theory itself are included here. And finally, in Chapter 10, I attempt to give a very brief summary of what can be legitimately abstracted from the fields of economics and the social sciences and where their insights might be used to guide educational policy in the United States. Of course, since I believe that educational policy is more frequently guided by the vested interests of different interest groups in society, I do not assume that my review will necessarily be seen as "correct" by any particular faction in the continuing debate over school reform. But I will try to clarify some of my assessments.

It will become clear that the scope of this book is rather complex in nature, especially given the space limitations I have set for the work. Given this, I have attempted to list at the end of each chapter additional works that more intensively deal with various aspects of particular themes developed within them. Should my remarks on any given topic prove difficult to decipher, please consult either the original sources noted, or these supplemental texts. I hope to inspire many of my readers to question seriously much of what passes for sound educational reform policy in the United States.

NOTES

1. National Commission on Excellence in Education, *A Nation at Risk: The Imperative for Educational Reform*. Washington, DC: U.S. Government Printing Office, 1983, pp. 1–2.
2. Carnegie Forum on Education and the Economy, *A Nation Prepared: Teachers for the 21st Century*. Washington, DC: Carnegie Commission, 1986, p. 2.

3. National Education Association, *Investing in America's Future: The Role of Public Education in Economic Growth and The American Defense Education Act.* Washington, DC: NEA, 1983, pp. 4, 30.
4. David T. Kearns, *An Education Recovery Plan for America.* Stamford, CT: Xerox Corporation, October 1987, p. 1.

CHAPTER 2

The Political Economy
of Economic Development
and Population Quality

A primary driving force behind much political and economic activity in Western nations these days is the concept of economic development. From New England to California, from Brazil to China, and virtually everywhere else, political and business leaders around the globe argue that human happiness, and satisfaction for their constituents, depends on more economic development and greater economic productivity. How will world hunger be solved? More economic development. How will poverty be erased? More economic development. How will the plight of various disenfranchised minority groups be alleviated? More economic development.

In some ways, this is a curious line of reasoning. Yet many currently respectable economists, many political leaders, and large numbers of the public are beginning to accept such arguments as true.

Similarly, since many current political and business leaders agree that more economic development will solve most of our problems, they likewise insist that factors potentially involved in enhancing such development need better understanding and more favorable government support. Tax policies, for example, have typically been a growing arena of interest among twentieth-century economists. One popular argument among economic advisors to former President Reagan was that income tax rates ought to be lowered significantly in the United States to aid in the process of increased economic development. Such an argument was theoretically made not in order to "be kind" to American taxpayers, but rather because it is argued that more money in the hands of investors and consumers aids in continued economic growth.

So, too, investing in "population quality" has become a favorite theme among some economists in the twentieth century. According to such reasoning, a more productive economy depends on a healthier and better educated citizenry. A strong economy demands better workers, and likewise, healthier and more skilled workers help to bring about a better economy. Therefore, according to proponents of modern day human capital theory, enhanced economic development demands government policies conducive to improved population quality. Governments concerned about the future of their economic growth ought to invest in hospitals, vocational education programs, public schools, and nutritional improvement campaigns if they seek either to remain economically viable and/or enter the ranks of nations already economically advanced.

Although notions that unlimited economic development is always good, and that government agencies ought to continuously aid in the economic development process seem almost the conventional wisdom today, this has not always been the case. Furthermore, while theories and models attempting to determine the economic value of humans with differing amounts and types of occupational skills have been around (and debated) for some time, arguments that state and/or national governments ought to be systematically involved in aiding the process of human capital formation are rather recent. And most importantly for our purposes, arguments that public schools ought to play a significant role in the process of economic development, through the development of human resources for the private sector, has also had its share of advocates and critics.

Because the intent of this book is to help educators and future educators critically examine much of the logic and policy proposals of current American school reform agendas, one logical starting place for investigation lies in the origin of arguments concerning the several important economic and educational themes just mentioned. In point of fact, theoretical disagreements about the value and desirability of economic development, the process of conceptualizing population quality, and the role of public education in the economic development process all have a long and interesting history.

THE POLITICAL ECONOMY
OF ECONOMIC GROWTH

Contemporary economics as an academic field has gone through a number of important transformations since its birth in the seventeenth century. Its beginning is typically placed at that time not because earlier scholars and writers had been uninterested in economic matters, but because it was during this period that scholars began to wonder about such abstract questions as the "meaning" of money and the origin of national wealth.

By the late eighteenth century, what are now recognized as legitimate findings and debates in economics were the focus of the field of political economy. Political economy was both an academic and an applied area of interest among classical economic thinkers like Adam Smith, David Ricardo, John Stuart Mill, and Karl Marx. Major conceptual concerns of such economists were the desirable economic development strategies of the European countries during this period. Unlike many current economists, however, who specialize in various investment or capital accumulation policies of particular businesses or governments, early political economists were also philosophers and political scientists.

In general, political economists were interested in understanding the economic laws that might benefit (or harm) material wealth and social development in Europe. Most believed that the progress of Western civilization depended on the rational development of market economies, as opposed to earlier feudal and/or church-dominated economic and political systems. The various types of research and scholarship undertaken by these writers from the end of the seventeenth century until at least the late nineteenth century dealt with attempts to understand the laws governing rational human economic behavior. Furthermore, most political economists believed their theories had important policy implications for European nation-states of the eighteenth and nineteenth century, and they were frequently called upon to advise business and political groups in their own countries.

By almost any account, Adam Smith was the leading theorist and spokesperson of late eighteenth- and early nineteenth-century capitalism. Even today, his most influential work, *The Wealth of Nations,* is used in beginning economics classes as one important explanation of how western economies do (or did) operate. As the title implies, Smith was convinced that a thorough understanding of the laws of economics would help explain how to improve both the material and the social conditions of his native England.

Like theorists of earlier economic schools, Smith was interested in the nature of wealth and how changes in the developing capitalist economies in western Europe would (or wouldn't) enhance it. However, he disagreed with several earlier political economists who had particularly emphasized either agricultural productivity or unrestricted trade. Rather, he argued that production of manufactured goods and the competition between individuals and companies to produce those goods was crucial to economic development. In a now classic summary of the historical development of economic thought, Robert Heilbroner writes:

> Adam Smith's laws of the market are basically simple. They tell us that the outcome of a certain kind of behavior in a certain social framework will bring about perfectly definite and foreseeable results. Specifically they

show us how the drive of individual self interest in an environment of similarly motivated individuals will result in competition; and they further demonstrate how competition will result in the provision of those goods that society wants, in the quantities that society desires, and at the prices society is willing to pay.[1]

As this passage suggests, early economists were not only interested in the nature of wealth and the mechanisms by which it could be accumulated, but were also vitally interested in the social and political consequences of economic development. For example, Smith was very concerned with social inequality and moral integration in his country and was convinced that the best economic, social, and moral course available for a nation lay in capitalist development. Unrestricted capitalism would not only increase individual standards of living and national wealth, but would provide for equality of opportunity inasmuch as workers would be free to sell their labor in competition with other workers. Efficiency concerns among businesses competing for their share of any consumer market would stimulate an increasing division of labor in society. Such occupational specialization would keep businesses efficient, thus driving down consumer costs.

By Smith's reckoning, then, an unrestrained and open capitalist system was the best of all possible worlds, where the very factors that allowed competition in the marketplace to flourish would yield reciprocally positive benefits for everyone's standard of living. Increased standards of living would make workers even better at their jobs, thus further stimulating economic productivity and national wealth.

EARLY CRITICS OF SMITH'S POLITICAL ECONOMY

While the elegant simplicity of *The Wealth of Nations* no doubt has enhanced its continued appeal in many quarters of western culture, other political economists who also favored capitalist development believed Smith's analysis was much too utopian and simplistic. For example, Thomas Malthus agreed that the wealth of nations was dependent on the laws of production elaborated upon by Smith, yet he was unconvinced that population quality among the masses would increase as Smith believed. While Smith argued that individual pursuit of self-interest allowed under capitalism would enable workers to rationally pursue opportunities conducive to the betterment of their own economic conditions, Malthus doubted seriously whether humans were reflective enough to logically plan their futures and argued that irrational forces operating among impoverished populations would doom the poor to ever-increasing levels of economic misery in the face of larger national prosperity.

Malthus in essence argued that the large numbers of the poor so visible in the England of his day were due to the their own patterns of procreation. Not only were indigents impoverished because they had few moral and/or productive talents with which to raise themselves from the ranks of the poor, but, because they continued to breed children whom they had no ability to feed and nurture, they only perpetuated their misery while negating any overall increase in population quality.

Another early nineteenth-century philosopher, political economist, and social activist who disagreed with much of Smith's analysis was Robert Owen. According to Owen, Smith's assumption about the fundamental "building block" of human cultures was in error, as were his prescriptions for bringing about the best kind of society. Specifically, Owen argued that Smith was wrong in believing that competition between self-motivated individuals would or could be the driving force behind social progress. Rather, he believed strongly that the family and the community were essential components of satisfactory human existence. Unfortunately, free-ing individuals so that they could pursue job opportunities actually meant that many would be forced to leave homes and communities in search of employment just to stay alive. Thus, while such an economic system might free individuals from the archaic authority patterns of another era, it also had several overwhelming liabilities. Economic historian Karl Polanyi assessed Owen's contribution to the growing economic development debate:

> [Owen] grasped the fact that what appeared primarily as an economic problem was essentially a social one. In economic terms the worker was certainly exploited: he did not get in exchange that which was his due. But important though this was, it was far from all. In spite of exploitation, he might have been financially better off than before. But a principal quite unfavorable to individual and general happiness was working havoc with his social environment, his neighborhood, his standing in the community, his craft; in a word, with those relationships to nature and man in which his economic existence was formerly embedded. The industrial revolution was causing a social dislocation of stupendous proportions, and the problem of poverty was merely the economic aspect of this event. Owen justly pronounced that unless legislative interference and direction counteracted these devastating forces, great and permanent evils would follow.[2]

In essence, Robert Owen was one of the first to argue that human identity was crucially involved with the individual's participation in family, community, and occupational groups. He further argued that advances in economic growth ought to proceed with the social needs of individuals in mind. In England, Owen argued for decades that the government ought to establish and support collective economic enterprises. In order to accomplish such cooperative ventures, Owen invested much of his own money in several collectively owned and operated communities such as New Lanark in Scotland, and later, New Harmony, Indiana.

Unlike many more modern economists, political economists of the early nineteenth century realized that bringing about increased economic development called for political understandings and political actions as well as economic ones. David Ricardo, another important political economist, argued that Smith's utopian economic system underestimated the entrenched forces that would resist an open market system. Ricardo reasoned that economic productivity was not based solely on consumer demand, but also on the costs of producing goods by manufacturers. Importantly, Ricardo argued that there existed a class of citizens within developing European nations who would and did profit enormously from capitalism, and yet contributed little to its growth. If anything, this class severely hampered economic development by continually raising the cost of production for manufacturers. These individuals were typically aristocrats who held title to much of the agricultural land in eighteenth- and nineteenth-century England.

Because it was in the interest of landholders to charge the most that they could for the use of their land, and because workers had to eat, wages of workers would always be spent on the food necessary to survive. If workers had no money to spend on products produced by growing industrial firms, consumer demand would necessarily remain marginal. Without consumer demand for manufactured products, there could be few opportunities for capitalist profits. Without profits, there could be little investment in future economic development. Without economic development, there could only be economic stagnation rather than economic growth. Obviously, population quality would also suffer or remain stagnant as a result.

For each of these several political economists then, Adam Smith's utopian system was seen as problematic. For Robert Owen, capitalism was seen as socially irresponsible. For Thomas Malthus, the potential benefits of capitalism would never reach the masses. And for David Ricardo, capitalist development would entail serious power shifts within the nation–state if it were ever to be put into practice.

THE POLITICAL ECONOMY OF KARL MARX

By far the most influential counterarguments to the social and political assumptions that lie behind classical economic theories like that of Adam Smith are to be found in the works of Karl Marx. For example, Marx agreed with Ricardo that vested interests of existing and emerging economic classes ensured continuous social conflict. And since the logic of capitalist growth called for ever-increasing development, capitalism as an economic mode would continue to provide a fertile ground for social unrest. Similiarly, Marx agreed with Owen that the social nature of humanity was sorely misunderstood by the supporters of capitalism who championed individual self-interest as the essential human characteristic. Rather, argued Marx, it was only in community with others that the individual could be whole, and thus an economic system that forced individuals to compete with each other for survival could never satisfy the essence of human nature.

Central to Marxist theory on the relationship between capitalist economic development and its implications for the individual was the concept of alienation. According to Marx, a fundamental distinction between humans and other animate species is the ability humans have to transform nature via the process of craftsmanship. By transforming nature through his or her labor, the craftspersons who make the resultant products (be they furniture from a tree, clothing from wool, or shoes from cowhide) can identify with them. Indeed, since much artisan production was carried out by families, household production units were in fact the cornerstones of economic life, and community social structure itself depended on a production system that many classical economists viewed as inefficient and archaic. According to Marx, then, the economic development systems proposed by classical economists were anti-individual and antisocial, and in essence would only serve those who eventually would come to own the factories and businesses, where individuals "freed" from family and community life would have to come to sell their labor.

Inasmuch as Marx was vitally interested in human equality and the creative forces of individuals, he rejected completely the political economy of Adam Smith and the other classical economists. Rather, he argued, the capitalist economic system and the new social order it would create would one day be replaced by socialism. Those economists calling for policies to enhance private enterprise as the mechanism for national economic growth and development were calling for the exploitation of workers on whose shoulders the costs of such development would fall. And since the only way to enhance the wealth of nations was to exploit one class of people for the gain of another, he viewed the then growing field of political economy as illegitimate. Furthermore, since by definition he believed capitalism inhumane and antisocial as well as exploitive, he argued that capitalism would one day fall under its own weight. In criticizing the classical economists of his day, Marx wrote:

> [When] economists define the relationship of wages to profit, they take the interests of capitalists as the basis; in other words, they take for granted what they should explain. Similarly, competition is accounted for by external circumstances. Political economy never tells us whether these external and seemingly accidental circumstances are perhaps a necessary development. To economists, exchange itself seems an accidental fact. The only moving forces that political economy recognizes are human greed and the war among the greedy—competition.[3]

JOHN STUART MILL

Lying conceptually between the ideas of the classical economists like Adam Smith and more critical interpretations like those of Karl Marx were the influential works of John Stuart Mill. Like the classical economists, he too was interested in the betterment of European society and believed that individual self-interest, freedom, and enlightment were essential human goals. As a political economist, Mill felt that there existed understandable laws governing the economic growth and development necessary for the fulfillment of individual desires and social uplift. However, while he was sure that there were natural laws that best predicted and explained production factors most conducive to such growth, he reasoned that there were no natural laws governing economic distribution.

Mill argued that capitalism on the whole was very desirable and should be politically facilitated. Yet he also noted that there were potential developments endemic to such a system that could be degrading and exploitive to human relationships. In such cases where the economic system proved unequal or provided less than satisfactory working conditions for workers, the economic distribution system could be used to help offset such deleterious practices. In other words, Mill argued that the distribution of economic surplus was not governed by the laws of nature, but rather by the laws established by society. Heilbroner summarizes Mill's position on these matters:

> economic laws of production concern nature. There is nothing arbitrary about whether labor is more productive in this use or that, nor is there anything capricious or optional about such economic phenomena as the diminishing powers of productivity of the soil. . . . But . . . once we have produced wealth as best we can, we can do with it as we like. . . . Society could tax and subsidize, it could expropriate and redistribute. It could give all its wealth to a king, or it could run a gigantic charity ward. . . . But whatever [society] did, there was no "correct" distribution—at least none that economics had any claim to fathom.[4]

POLITICAL ECONOMISTS' VIEWS ON POPULATION QUALITY AND PUBLIC EDUCATION

Competing views of the classical economists on goals and processes of economic development have been presented here for two reasons. First, it is important for the reader to understand that very serious disagreements between economists did and still do exist. Conflicting perspectives on the nature and desirability of western capitalism are still debated among economists, regardless of what one reads in the local newspaper or hears from various political leaders.

Second, while today's "conventional wisdom" is that economic development ought rightfully to be the aim of the public school, most of the early champions of capitalism did not make such arguments in their writings. On the one hand, public education as we know it today did not exist in Europe until long after the works mentioned here were produced. Rather, formal schooling in England and in Europe was conducted either in private institutions or in various types of religiously sponsored charity institutions. Most children did not go to public school at all. Furthermore, private education for the elite purposely avoided training wealthy children for the emerging industrial order. Following in the Judeo-Christian tradition, private school curricula typically focused on moral, religious, and philosophical instruction rather than occupational training. The still popular classical model of education inherited from the Greeks, for example, was seen as a process of developing one's reasoning abilities. And such pursuits could be undertaken only when unencumbered by vocational needs.

On the other hand, many classical economists believed that the wealth of national economies and the economic value of individuals to their nations depended on the different amounts and types of skills people possessed. William Petty, for example, attempted to quantify the economic power of various European nations one hundred years before Adam Smith (that is, in the mid-seventeenth century). In this assessment, he developed a very rudimentary formula for estimating the economic value of national populations to national wealth. Given the average contribution of wage earners to national economies, Petty also gave estimates of economic costs incurred to nations as the result of war casualties and other forms of premature death.[5]

In the following two centuries other attempts were made to improve upon Petty's earlier, less sophisticated theories. William Farr, for example, was interested in devising a new tax scheme in England that would target not only an individual's material wealth, but also the value of an individual's skills. He argued that the productive value of people with specific types of skills could be predicted over their lifetimes, and thus legitimate tax rates applied to their economic value in society.[6]

While Farr's calculations continued the earlier interest in assessing the value of human skills within national economies, it naturally had certain policy limitations. For example, it would appear difficult to tax workers in the present for income they might generate in the future, even assuming the methods used in calculating such figures were accurate. Nevertheless, during the nineteenth century other economists began to take an interest in assessing the value of wage earners, not necessarily because they were interested in national economic development issues, but frequently because court cases involving wrongful death litigation needed projections of future earnings potential in settlement claims.

In essence, then, there appears to be little doubt that classical economists believed that human skill levels were important and ought to figure in calculations of economic development. However, the way that humans acquired occupational skills was rarely discussed, and notions that governments ought to take an active role in helping to train future workers were rarely advanced by the political economists. It was typically assumed that workers learned their future trades either within their family settings, or in apprenticeship to other craftsmen. Furthermore, since most political economists were advocates of competition in the marketplace, they typically argued against government intervention in the dynamics of the private sector. Governments ought not to become involved in occupational training for needs of particular industries, because such subsidized programs might give unfair advantage to some firms over others.

Significantly, Adam Smith had opinions about both the importance of population quality and worker skills in the economic development process and about desirable goals for state financed educational institutions. And contrary to what some might suspect, they had little in common. For example, Smith agreed that worker skills were a key component of economic development, as were other population quality factors. However, the improvement of population quality for Smith was an outcome or benefit of the economic system he championed, and such benefits would further enhance economic development as workers became healthier and more proficient. Relatedly, the specialization that would increasingly be demanded in the workplace would lead to more precise and efficient skill acquisition by workers and would be acquired on the job, not at the public expense.

Yet, for Smith the acquisition of skills relevant to the economic development process was not to be confused with objectives of public education, assuming public schools ever became available. Smith argued, in fact, that the process of economic development and the division of labor in capitalist society would have negative consequences for human intellectuality, which education might hopefully counteract. According to Smith, in *The Wealth of Nations:*

> In the progress of the division of labor, the employment of the far greater part of those who live by labor, that is, of the greater body of the people, comes to be confined to a very few simple operations, frequently to one or two. But the understandings of the greater part of men are necessarily formed by their ordinary employments. The man whose whole life is spent in performing a few simple operations, of which the effects too are, perhaps, always the same, or very nearly the same, has no occasion to exert his understanding, or to exercise his invention in finding out expedients for removing difficulties which never occur. He naturally loses, therefore, the habit of such exertion, and generally becomes as stupid and ignorant as it is possible for a human creature to become. The torpor of his

mind renders him, not only incapable of relishing or bearing a part in any rational conversation, but of conceiving any generous, noble, or tender sentiment, and consequently of forming any just judgement concerning many even of the ordinary duties of private life. . . . His dexterity at his own particular trade seems, in this manner, to be acquired at the expense of his intellectual, social, and martial values.[7]

For Smith then, were there to be public expenditure for mass education it should be accomplished to enlighten workers intellectually and to provide for citizenship education. And if anything, education was seen as desirable to counterbalance the stupifying effects of occupational specialization, rather than to precede, augment, or extend it.

Robert Owen was also greatly interested in the possibilities of public education, especially for the poor and working class. However, Owen believed that achieving human happiness demanded some critical assessments of the human possibilities and problems of economic development then occurring in England. He argued that classical notions of individual "enlightenment" were also too limited a curricular base for helping workers and the poor to understand the incredible social and economic changes going on around them.

Owen argued that, as long as individuals were pitted against each other in economic competition, poverty, crime, war, and other immoral pursuits would flourish and grow even within a supposedly healthy economy. This would be so, he argued, because many if not most of the leaders as well as the workers and the poor in early nineteenth-century England had themselves been mis-educated. He argued that economic development strategies ought to be socially responsible and should help bring about a society in which the greatest number of individuals were simultaneously satisfied. He claimed that it was in everyone's best interest to be concerned with the happiness of others, not just with achieving individual success.

For John Stuart Mill, too, the material benefits of capitalism were not to be confused with moral and ethical development of the individual or of human society. For Mill, economic development would allow for the further realization of individual satisfaction, intellectual growth, and the perfection of social institutions in which individuals could grow and prosper. Very unlike Owen, however, Mill suggested that the needs of the economy and the needs of democracy were not always the same. Economic development was to be used by humans to help perfect their society, but the science of economics did not and could not specify how humans should live their lives. Such matters had to remain in the province of moral and ethical analyses and were available within the Western liberal tradition. Speaking of the limits of technical education and in favor of a more general one, Mills argued:

Men are men before they are lawyers or physicians or merchants or manufacturers; and if you make them capable and sensible men, they will make themselves capable and sensible lawyers and physicians. What professional men should carry away with them from a university is not professional knowledge, but that which should direct the use of their professional knowledge and bring the light of general culture to illuminate the technicalities of a special pursuit. Men may be competent lawyers without general education, but it depends on general education to make them philosophic lawyers—who demand, and are capable of apprehending, principles, instead of merely cramming their head with details. And so of all other useful pursuits, mechanical included. Education makes a man a more intelligent shoemaker, if that be his occupation, but not by teaching him to make shoes; it does so by the mental excercise it gives and the habits it impresses.[8]

Believing himself that occupational skills were an important component of economic development, Mills still rejected the suggestion that occupational specialization ought to monopolize the learning objectives of public education:

Government and civil society are the most complicated of all subjects accessible to the human mind; and he who would deal competently with them as a thinker, and not as a blind follower of a party, requires not only a general knowledge of the leading facts of life, both moral and material, but an understanding exercised and disciplined in the principles and rules of sound thinking up to a point which neither the experience of life nor any one science or branch of knowledge affords.[9]

MARX'S CRITIQUE OF EDUCATIONAL POSSIBILITIES UNDER CAPITALISM

Karl Marx criticized the feasibility of educational models like those put forth by men like Mills, Owen, and Smith. For Marx, the driving force behind capitalist expansion was to continually seek ways of driving down the costs of human labor involved in the manufacturing process. One important way to accomplish this end was to continually reduce the content of skilled occupations to more menial tasks. In this way, less talented workers could be used in production processes, because they would demand lower wages for their work. Since many potential workers either had been or could quickly be given the few occupational skills necessary to run machines or complete very simple operations, the competition for even such marginal jobs would be intense outside the factory gates.

Thus, contrary to conventional wisdom, Adam Smith agreed with Marx on the potentially deleterious effect of the workplace on the intellectual development of workers. What they disagreed on was the occupational "benefits" of the division of labor for human skill enhancement, Smith arguing that worker specialization was economically advantageous and a prerequisite to meeting consumer needs, Marx that specialization was alienating and might facilitate consumer needs of the wealthy, but not of the working class.

Furthermore, argued Marx, other population quality factors such as the general health and nutrition of workers would decline rather than be improved under capitalism for all but the owners of the means of production, which is to say, for most of the population of any developing capitalist country. In order to stay in business, according to Marx, factory owners would have to pay just enough to workers to keep them alive. And in the meantime, such owners would have to keep finding new ways to replace workers (thus keeping them unemployed) with more advanced technologies.

So too, argued Marx, all government funded institutions (like the school) would inevitably have to conform to demands of the private sector in order to operate. Marx argued that public funds for the social and educational needs of workers would not be forthcoming in the future as Smith and several other political economists had hoped. Because capitalists were locked into epic struggles among themselves for control of their shares of the market, and because representatives of this social class would come to dominate all political offices due to their financial power, the common people would never see any public benefit for their contribution to economic development.

Rather, capitalists through their official government channels would utilize the state to put into practice economic and social policies seen as beneficial to their own class interests, that is, policies designed to further legitimate and extend the possibilities for capitalist economic development. There would be no questioning of the free enterprise system or of the importance of property ownership. Ideas skeptical toward capitalism would not be entertained in government-financed institutions, for such ideas might question the emerging power base of capitalism itself.

SUMMARY

The field of economics as it exists today had many of its intellectual origins in the writings of European political economists of the late eighteenth and early nineteenth century. Central to the works of these political economists was their conviction that economic development depended on a free market system where goods and services could be efficiently produced. Although some political economists could see only good coming out of such a system for all individuals, others were less optimistic. In this chapter I have tried to briefly review several of the important debates among these writers.

Most political economists tended to agree that human skills were important components of economic development, and that better-skilled workers aided in the process of economic growth. On the other hand, some writers (like Malthus) were unsure that expanding economic opportunities would improve everyone's standard of living, and some (like Owen and Marx) contended that skill enhancement through the division of labor would have various harmful consequences in the long run.

Conspicuous by its absence in much of classical economics literature is any discussion of the actual process whereby people acquired their occupational skills. Furthermore, since relatively few public educational systems were established in Europe at the time the political economists were writing (e.g., in Prussia from the eighteenth century, in France from the nineteenth century), rarely, if ever, was there much discussion of the advantages for economic development of such systems. Interestingly, those classical economists who did propose or support public instruction believed their mission ought to transcend education for economic development and ought rather to concentrate on political, social, and citizenship issues. It would primarily remain to future economists, social scientists, educators, and political leaders to make specific arguments linking the purpose of public education with economic development objectives.

NOTES

1. Robert Heilbroner, *The Wordly Philosophers*. New York: Simon & Schuster, 1967 (3rd. edition), pp. 49–50.
2. Karl Polanyi, *The Great Transformation: The Political and Economic Origins of Our Time*. Boston: Beacon Press, 1957, p. 129.
3. Karl Marx, "Alienated Labor," in E. Josephson and M. Josephson (eds.), *Man Alone: Alienation in Modern Society*. New York: Dell, 1962, pp. 93–94.
4. Heilbroner, *Worldly Philosophers,* pp. 118–119.
5. Charles Hull (ed.), *The Economic Writings of Sir William Petty,* vol. 1 and 2. Cambridge: University of Cambridge, 1899.
6 William Farr, "Equitable Taxation of Property," *Journal of the Royal Statistical Society,* 16 (March), 1853: 1–45.
7. Adam Smith, *An Inquiry into the Nature and Causes of The Wealth of Nations*. New York: Modern Library, 1937, pp. 734–735.
8. John Stuart Mill, "Inaugural Address at the University of St. Andrews," in Francis Garforth (ed.), *John Stuart Mill on Education*. New York: Teachers College Press, 1971, p. 156.
9. *Ibid.,* p. 166.

FOR ADDITIONAL READING

In addition to the works by Adam Smith and John Stuart Mill listed in the Notes, several other original sources are worthy of inspection. Thomas Malthus's views on the "population problem" are available in his work *On*

Population (New York: Random House, 1960). John Stuart Mill's *Principles of Political Economy* (New York: Longmans, Green & Co., 1909) also elaborates more fully on his economic analysis than does the educationally focused collection previously cited. For some exposure to Marx's own writings, I would recommend the edited collection by Robert Freedman entitled *Marx on Economics* (New York: Harcourt & Brace, 1961). In addition, a brief but insightful contemporary overview of Marxist theory is available in Peter Worsley's *Marx and Marxism* (New York: Tavistock Publications, 1982). For an overview and samples of Robert Owen's work, I suggest his own *Life of Robert Owen* (New York: Alfred A. Knopf, 1920).

On the other hand, some original works by classical political economists are quite difficult to read. David Ricardo's original works fall into this category, and, for an overview of his perspectives (and those of several others) on economic development, I have found the book by K. Cole, J. Cameron, and C. Edwards *Why Economists Disagree: The Political Economy of Economics* (New York: Longman, 1983) quite helpful. Another secondary source that specifically investigates the contrasting perspectives of political economists on human capital formation is available in the essay by B.F. Kiker entitled "The Historical Roots of the Concept of Human Capital" (*Journal of Political Economy,* 74 (5), 1966: 481–499). In addition to the comprehensive overviews of the evolution of capitalist economic thought provided by Robert Heilbroner and Karl Polanyi, I have found the prologue of Randall Collin's *Three Sociological Traditions* (New York: Oxford University Press, 1985) very informative.

CHAPTER 3

Education, Character Training, and Economic Development in Nineteenth-Century America

Current calls for school reform typically equate national economic progress with the structure of schooling opportunities and standards. Occupational and vocational skills are argued to be an essential component of our present and future economic health, and American public schools are increasingly seen as the focal point for upgrading human resources via the teaching of such skills. However, prior to the common school movement of the mid-nineteenth century, education for economic development was not a common theme in this country. Rather, several intellectual, moral, and political agendas were advocated by those interested in the possibilities of education.

With the coming of industrialization, a number of educational advocates became interested in the vocational possibilities of education. Arguments linking economic development with the purposes of *public* schooling during its early years, however, focused not so much on the cognitive skills necessary for employment, but on continuing the earlier emphasis on moral instruction and character training as prerequisites for individual success in the private sector. On the other hand, by the end of the nineteenth century, the economic and social possibilities of the school were widely discussed, and curricular efforts directly linking public schooling objectives with requirements of the business world were increasingly put into place. This chapter describes how the logic of education for economic development had its origins in public education and examines the development of this linkage during the nineteenth century.

It should be pointed out, of course, that formal education has typically been viewed with some suspicion by many Americans. Many citizens of this country viewed "book learning" as elitist in the eighteenth and early nineteenth centuries. Some still do. A sound practical education learned at home and religious education available in church were typically all that children were thought to need in rural America. Classical or liberal arts education was generally the curriculum of private secondary schools and colleges, and those who primarily undertook such instruction were from wealthy families and slated for elite positions in law or politics. As mentioned earlier, classical notions of education emphasized intellectual refinement and the development of reasoning abilities. Education was championed by many American elites as independent of work, and an activity to be pursued for intellectual, moral, and political reasons, not because its content was directly vocationally relevant.

EARLY VISIONS AND DEBATES ABOUT THE GOALS OF AMERICAN EDUCATION

In the United States, as elsewhere, state mandated public education did not exist prior to the nineteenth century. As in much of England, America was primarily a rural nation in the seventeenth, eighteenth, and early nineteenth centuries, and rural, local schools run by parents and trustees were the norm wherever there were any schools at all. And even when schools may have been provided in much of rural America, attendance figures suggest much less participation by children at that time than we have now. This is not to suggest, however, that the concept of education was unimportant in our early history. In point of fact, there were at least two very powerful arguments linking educational goals with the moral and political success of our country prior to the coming of the common school in the mid-nineteenth century.

One early curricular concern adults had for children in America was for their moral instruction. This interest dated to the seventeenth century and was concentrated upon exposure to Christian morality and the teaching of the Bible. A Massachusetts law requiring parents to teach their children how to read (the Bible) was the first educational legislation passed in what would later become the United States. The intent of this law, entitled the "Old Deluder Satan" Act, was to teach children right from wrong; and to keep them from falling into temptation through study of the word of God.

Christianity would remain a strong curricular force in adult ambitions for their children's education throughout the seventeenth and eighteenth centuries. As the educational historian Henry Perkinson phrased it:

> Alone in the savage wilderness of their new settlements, the earliest colonists had to rely upon schools and schoolteachers far more than they

did in Europe. Forced to spend their days securing the basic necessities of life, these pioneer parents had little time to care for their children. Moreover, since their New World lacked the agencies of civilization commonplace in the mother country, parents in the New World feared that their children, if untended, might degenerate into savagery—not an unlikely fate in this strange, wild, and dangerous land. . . . Thus it happened that the first compulsory education laws of modern times appeared in the least civilized part of the Western world and, in fact, were a product of the very lack of civilization.[1]

Even in the nineteenth century, Christianity was an extremely important force in helping to bring about public education. According to educational historians David Tyack and Elizabeth Hansot, the Sunday School Movement that grew rapidly during the early nineteenth century was one of several important precursors to the common school of the mid-nineteenth century.[2] Yet, another, more secular and political concern began to have important consequences for educational planning and interests by the turn of the nineteenth century.

EDUCATION FOR DEMOCRACY
AND POLITICAL LEADERSHIP

Immediately following the American War of Independence, many of America's emerging leaders became concerned about the political requirements necessary to sustain and enhance our new democracy. In just a brief matter of time, many such leaders began to talk about the necessity of formally instructing children in the rights and duties of American citizenship.

Again, the possibility of infusing existing and typically voluntary rural schools with a new curricular focus on patriotism and our new system of government did not depend upon how such a curriculum would be related to economic development. In fact, politics and, specifically, democratic forms of government were already widely studied subjects among America's elite academies. Furthermore, those who had studied the political philosophy of earlier civilizations knew that education played an important role in those societies' democratic success. Education, for example, was claimed to be the foundation of democracy in ancient Athens, where it was argued to be the duty of (free) male citizens to think logically, speak effectively and read analytically. Only in such a way, it was believed, could democracy flourish:

The education of a free man, in contrast to the training of an artisan or slave, centered in grammar, rhetoric, and logic, with some attention also to mathematics, music, literature, and the sciences. The purpose of such an education was not to prepare a man for some economic vocation, but to prepare him for the moral life in which he used his disciplined intelligence in making choices affecting his nation, his family, and himself.[3]

It is also important to note that many of the early political leaders concerned about the teaching of democracy and the enhancing of educational institutions in which such topics could be pursued did so on secular rather than religious grounds. Pronouncements about the desirability and viability of the new American government and the justification for political decision making were frequently made on rational grounds that were not necessarily rooted in religious tradition. For example, both religious *and* secular justifications for declaring independence from England are visible in the second paragraph of the Declaration of Independence. Note that while human rights are endowed by the "Creator," the securing of such rights demands participation of the public in evaluating and potentially creating for themselves the political apparatus for doing so:

We hold these truths to be self-evident, that all men are created equal, that they are endowed by their Creator with certain unalienable rights, that among these are life, liberty, and the pursuit of happiness. That, to secure these rights, governments are instituted among men, deriving their just powers from the consent of the governed. That, whenever any form of government becomes destructive of these ends, it is the right of the people to alter or abolish it, and to institute new government, laying its foundation on such principles, and organizing its powers in such form, as to them shall seem most likely to effect their safety and happiness.

Another good example of the secular hopes for the possibilities of public schooling in such a regard is visible in the early educational proposals of Thomas Jefferson for his own state:

Flush with the enthusiasm and the anxieties of new nationhood, Thomas Jefferson proposed for Virginia a three-tiered system of local education—free elementary schools, twenty regional academies with free tuition for selected boys, and support at William and Mary College for the best ten needy academy graduates. . . . In the preamble of [this] 1779 bill for free schools in Virginia, [he] laid out the basic logic of state-sponsored schools for republican citizenship. Citizens must choose leaders wisely, defeat ambition and corruption in politics, and protect liberty by keeping a vigilant eye on government. All citizens should have a chance not only to vote but to be elected. The government needed wise and honest laws, Jefferson argued, and thus it needs educated and virtuous lawmakers. . . . [Such] features were unheard of before Jefferson's proposals of 1779.[4]

LINKING EDUCATIONAL
OPPORTUNITIES WITH SCHOOLING:
THE RISE OF TUITION ACADEMIES

Even given the social ferment just preceding and directly following the Revolutionary War, and even given the fact that most Americans coming to the New World in the seventeenth and eighteenth century were (Protestant) Christians, most Americans were still unwilling to sponsor extensive public schooling projects around the nation designed to instruct children on such matters. Religion could be learned at home and in the church. Learning about democracy and politics might be important, but its principles could be learned just as well in the home and in community meetings. To study anything, after all, still seemed like an activity for the wealthy, not one for farmers or small scale entrepreneurs.

Prior at least to the 1820s, compelling arguments against state provision of public schooling (except for the poorest of children) ruled the day. Rural Americans needed practical and hands-on knowledge to earn a living in the fields, and they likewise needed their children's help there. Furthermore, the talents rural children would need as adults were themselves to be developed either in the home, in apprenticeship, or on the farm. Learning to read and to write was important, as was some knowledge of our emerging political system. But such objectives, it was thought, could easily be attained by children in the home after the day's work was complete—or in the local school when the growing season was over for the year. Before the Industrial Revolution, in other words, there were very few Americans who viewed schooling of any kind as relevant to occupational success and/or economic development. Or at least this was the assessment made by the educational historian Carl Kaestle:

> As with religion and politics, the notion that economic development would have an effect on education would seem plausible, but the facts are obscure. It seems logical that wider geographical horizons, more impersonal markets, more printed communication, and a gradually increasing proportion of wage-earning workers in the labor market would foster the development of schooling for literacy, morality, and a more mobile world. But explicit connections between economic development and education were infrequent and vague. Nowhere was the contribution of education to economic growth emphasized or spelled out in detail. Even in the political economy treatises written by Americans in the 1820s and 1830s, education was a minor theme. If education was an ingredient in expansive capitalism, the connection escaped capitalists in the early national period.[5]

On the other hand, throughout the eighteenth century a specialized school form had existed in several growing towns and cities. One of

America's economic development "problems" in its relatively few cities during this period was that vocational opportunities for accountants, surveyors, clerks, and so on grew faster than the number of people who could fill them. And, as such "high technology" jobs had few traditional training programs or avenues into them, this period saw a growing number of private educational institutions dedicated to training boys specifically for them. Significantly, these tuition academies were of a much more occupationally oriented nature than the majority of private schools, which still focused on the liberal arts.

> Throughout the late seventeenth and the eighteenth centuries private "adventure" schools had sprung up in all of the Eastern towns and cities. These schools usually consisted of one teacher, who provided instruction in a great number of "modern subjects": commerical subjects, including arithmetic, accounting, bookkeeping, penmanship, letter writing; pure and applied mathematics, including engineering, surveying, navigation; [and] modern foreign languages. . . .[6]

While the actual numbers of students who could afford to attend such institutions were few, the fact remains that there did exist a number of private schools organized and operated on the premise that they could train boys for emerging occupations. Such a fact also suggests how profoundly emerging professional trades in urban areas might alter notions about the occupational aspects of schooling in the years to come.

> The academy movement in North America was primarily a result of the desire to provide a more utilitarian education as compared with the education provided in classical grammar schools. . . . In North America, these institutions served two needs: They provided a useful [i.e., *rational*] education and at the same time they transmitted the [*secular*] culture required for entrance into the middle class. In other words, they were institutions that could provide social mobility for the average citizen.[7]

FROM A RURAL AMERICA TO AN URBAN ONE

By the early nineteenth century, then, at least four distinct educational philosophies or models were available in the United States. There were those who saw a need for children to be instructed in Protestant morality; those who believed an understanding of democracy was essential for all citizens; those who still maintained a liberal arts education was desirable; and a few who foresaw a need or demand for specialized professional training in urban areas. None of these "models," however, seemed to generate a movement for significant public school reform in America before

1820 or 1830. Schools did exist in the countryside, yet they were frequently haphazardly attended and run by local parents, rather than by any sort of educationally trained professionals with larger commitments to the school's utility in bringing about economic development and/or helping to institute social change. By the middle of the nineteenth century, however, capitalist economic development had begun to affect America's already established cities, and to help create a number of new ones (see Table 3.1).

With America's move from a rural precapitalist society to an industrial capitalist one, several important events occurred. On the one hand, country folk seeking improved occupational opportunities began to relocate into what had been small towns at a rapid pace. And as previously rural Americans had little experience in city building, such rapid demographic changes led to many new urban problems. With regard to children in the growing urban areas, several particular problems quickly emerged. One was that the social institutions that used to educate and shelter children (e.g., family relatives, local churches, etc.) were unavailable. As opposed to the rule in rural areas, children were not invited into work "settings" in the cities.

Many Americans who came to the cities to undertake factory work in mid-nineteenth-century America were the poorest of the rural areas. Prominent businessmen in industrializing cities perceived that many such children were uneducated at best, or uncivilized at worst; whatever their "academic" capabilities might have been, the character traits children would need to get a job in the future would remain undeveloped among these former residents of the countryside. To compound matters, soon other types of families and other types of children began to appear in newly urbanized America. These were immigrants, frequently not only from non-English-speaking countries, but *rural* immigrants from non-English-speaking countries. And in "extreme" cases, these immigrants were non-English-speaking, rural, and non-Protestant!

Much concern therefore gripped many civic and business leaders in industrial America: what to do with the children. One solution to this

TABLE 3.1. CITY GROWTH IN THE MID-NINETEENTH CENTURY

	1820	1860
Places of 5,000 to 10,000	22	136
Places of 10,000 to 25,000	8	58
Places of 25,000 to 50,000	2	19
Places of 50,000 to 100,000	1	7
Places over 100,000	1	9

(Source: U.S. Bureau of the Census, Historical Statistics, 14, 139, 427, as quoted by David B. Tyack, The One Best System: A History of American Urban Education [Cambridge, MA: Harvard University Press, 1974].)

problem was to employ older children and put them to work alongside their parents. After all, in rural settings children typically worked alongside adults. And in preindustrial America, boys and girls beyond the age of 10 or 12 were no longer considered children anyway. Yet, as time progressed, this tactic proved ineffective. Parents frequently objected to the harsh working conditions their children often faced, and other would-be workers were opposed to the fact that children were taking jobs they needed. This strategy did not solve the problem of younger children, or the problem of English instruction for young immigrants. And there was great fear that poor children who had few work habits necessary for employment, could not speak English, and/or who had little opportunity to learn about the political history and value of the United States might never be able to achieve the success that nineteenth-century American leaders began to equate with the promise of capitalist economic development.

THE COMMON SCHOOL SOLUTION

Urban leaders therefore found themselves with numerous social problems as a function of rapid American economic development in the mid-nineteenth century. Among them was the problem of instilling in all children the values and character traits necessary for employment in industrial settings (frequently including the study of English) and of helping them learn about how ever-expanding economic development would ultimately lead to the good life for everyone (according to Adam Smith's predictions).

Furthermore, most American business leaders seemed to concur that our potential for economic development was even better than that of England, because we were a young and vigorous nation, with no history of aristocracy or other archaic traditions to stand in the way of economic advance. In fact, many began to believe that the combination of our wealth of natural resources, democratic form of government, and sound Protestant heritage could not have happened by chance: America's past and future success must be a function of God's blessing upon us. Therefore, with courage, hard work, and initiative, the temporary social problems then blocking American advance could be quickly solved. The solution to the problem of educating urban American children for their future role in this nation's unfolding process of economic development was the common school.

The Common School Movement that took place in America's cities between 1840 and 1880 was undoubtedly a great success. School reformers during this period argued that the voluntary and unprofessional nature of rural community education would not do for America's industrial and urban areas, particularly given the influx of poor rural and immigrant children. A central element of arguments used by the "founding fathers" of American public education (e.g., Henry Barnard, Horace Mann, John Philbrick, etc.) was that public schooling in the future would be essential for the economic possibilities of both the individual and the nation. No longer would apprenticeship systems or family members be able to provide the education necessary for most young people to become successful in America.

The writings and speeches of Horace Mann, for example, provide good illustrations of arguments linking the social, political and economic benefits of compulsory education to the theme of economic development. As a native of Massachusetts, Mann grew up and lived in the most industrial of American states in the early capitalist period. Able to view the important economic transformations going on around him and the dramatic consequences such changes had on the lives of people in a rapidly urbanizing region, Mann was instrumental in persuading the Massachusetts legislature to establish a six-month minimum school year in that state in 1839. Later in his career, Mann served in the U.S. House of Representatives, where he was active in the antislavery movement, and finally as a college president and lecturer on political economy and moral philosophy. Throughout his career, education and its relationship to political economy (or how to advance the cause of economic development) were his most important themes.

For example, Mann argued that economic development in America had helped to usher in a new age of prosperity, yet at the same time had brought about a new imperative for an institutional setting designed to "civilize" children from all social classes. Mann believed, in other words, that capitalist economic development had the potential to improve every American's standard of living. However, the development of human resources for both national growth and for equalizing individual life opportunities could no longer be left to chance: the attainment of such objectives called for a mass public educational system:

> The arts of civilization have so multiplied the harvests of the earth, that a general famine will not again lend its aid to free the community of its surplus members. Society at large has emerged from that barbarian and semi-barbarian state where pestilence formerly had its birth, and committed its ravages. These great outlets and sluice-ways, which, in former times, relieved nations of the dregs and refuse of their population, being now closed, whatever want or crime we engender, or suffer to exist, we must live with. Whatever children, then, we suffer to grow up amongst us, we must live with as men; and our children must be their contemporaries. . . . [therefore] in a government like ours, each individual must think of the welfare of the State, as well as of the welfare of his own family, and therefore, of the children of others as well as his own.[8]

While much of Mann's appeal was to the public at large, he particularly directed his appeal toward the value of compulsory education for the private sector. Well-schooled people, he argued, would be more productive workers and would help create more wealth than uneducated ones:

> For the creation of wealth, then,—for the existence of a wealthy people and a wealthy nation,—intelligence is the grand condition. The number of improvers will increase as the intellectual constituency, if I may so call it, increases. . . . That political economy, therefore, which busies itself about capital and labor, supply and demand, interests and rents, favorable balances of trade, but leaves out of account the element of widespread mental development, is nought but stupendous folly. The greatest of all the arts in political economy is to change a consumer into a producer; and the next greatest is to increase the producer's producing power,—an end to be directly attained by increasing his intelligence.[9]

CHARACTER TRAINING AND THE COMMON SCHOOL

While many mid-nineteenth-century school reformers were convinced that well-thought-out educational institutions could aid in the process of economic development, their arguments were typically very different from those heard today. On the one hand, for example, the cognitive skills thought essential for future economic development by Mann and his cohorts were less frequently emphasized than the character training that they believed future enterprise entailed. If the schools could help produce individuals willing to work hard, obey authority, and respect America's new democratic way of life, then most specific vocational skills would develop as children went out into the world. Financial success and the creation of wealth for Horace Mann, for example, was not an end in itself. There were many economically successful yet unprincipled business leaders already in the private sector, and an important objective he sought for the schools was to ensure that the abuses of wealth would not continue in the future. Compulsory public education would not only provide avenues of economic opportunity for all citizens, but would also emphasize the moral instruction necessary for future Americans to avoid potential self-aggrandizement and greed—which the unbridled quest for financial success could engender:

> The more I see of our present civilization, and of the only remedies for its evils, the more I dread intellectual eminence, when separated from virtue. We are a sick world, for whose maladies the knowledge of truth, and obedience to it, are the only healing. . . . Surely nothing but universal education can counterwork [the] tendency to the domination of capital and servility of labor. If one class possess all the wealth and the education, while the residue of society is ignorant and poor, it matters not by what name the relation between them may be called: the latter, in fact and in truth, will be the servile dependents and subjects of the former. But if education be equally diffused, it will draw property after it by the

strongest of all attractions; for such a thing never did happen, and never can happen, as that an intelligent and practical body of men should be permanently poor. Property and labor in different classes are essentially antagonistic; but property and labor in the same class are essentially fraternal.[10]

Arguments like those offered by Horace Mann became increasingly persuasive between 1840 and the end of the Civil War. According to such logic, the future of America depended on economic development. Such development, in turn, was frequently argued as that which God had intended for the nation and was in accord with individuals' rational pursuit of happiness. The occasional abuses of capitalism noted by prominent school reformers were seen as a function of perhaps too rapid and too competitive a growth pattern. Thus, schooling was increasingly argued to be of benefit both for extending the system and for correcting some of its problems.

Besides hoping to extend the possibilities of economic development, those who labored on behalf of the Common School Movement also believed in the importance of justice and equality. Crusaders for the public school in America therefore saw their efforts and their success in economic, moral, and political terms. The school was argued to be an important panacea for enhancing economic development, providing social mobility, extending the blessings of liberty, and defending our democratic way. Such grand hopes for public education are clearly visible in two verses of Samuel Francis Smith's patriotic 1831 song *America,* which most of us still sing:

My country 'tis of thee
Sweet Land of Liberty,
    Of thee I sing;
Land where my fathers died,
Land of the Pilgrim's pride,
From every mountainside
    Let freedom ring.

Our glorious Land today
'Neath Education's sway
    Soars upward still.
Its halls of learning fair;
Whose bounties all may share,
Behold them everywhere
    On vale and hill.

Thy safeguard, Liberty,
Our School shall ever be;
    Our nation's pride.
No tyrant hand shall smite,
While with encircling might
All here are taught the Right
    With Truth Allied.

THE CHARACTER TRAITS OF EDUCATORS

Because the role of the school was not only to teach basic literacy skills to children, but to instruct them in the Protestant-inspired democratic character traits deemed necessary for success, teachers in America's growing urban centers were hired more for quality of character than for intellectual prowess. After all, the best way to *teach* children how to behave is to *show* them how to behave. Or at least this was the philosophy of administrators in most urban school districts. Public school teachers throughout the nineteenth century were as much selected for their image as for their knowledge. Female teachers for school-age children were almost always preferable, because they were typified as more refined and morally upright than men. The slightest hint that such teachers had become "contaminated" in the ways of the world (by getting married or having children) frequently led to their dismissal.

The importance of Protestant virtue also extended to the ranks of (typically male) school administrators, who ostensibly displayed the qualities of businessmen, but were also perceived as morally upright and pious community leaders. Many, if not most, school leaders during the critical phases of school reform were visibly active in local religious affairs or had come from clearly identified religious backgrounds. And naturally, being visible in civic and religious circles was clearly an advantage for school administrators throughout the early common school period.

COMBINING CHARACTER TRAINING
WITH COGNITIVE INSTRUCTION

Just how essential character building was for the mission of the common school is also suggested in the use and success of the most widely read school textbooks of the nineteenth century, the McGuffey readers. First published between 1836 and 1838, the McGuffey series included a speller, a primer, and four readers. In the first fourteen years after their initial release, and coinciding closely with the formative years of the common school movement, approximately 7 million books were sold. Between 1870 and 1890, when common schooling had penetrated most of the metropolitan areas of the United States, over 60 million were sold. Given the relatively small number of children in school during this period (compared with today's enrollment figures), such sales were quite astonishing.

The moral instruction and examples of character traits to be prized in the McGuffey readers approximate very closely the curricular aims of public instruction that Horace Mann was championing at the legislative level. According to another educational historian, Richard Mosier:

The great concern of the readers is not the abundant economic individualism or the cruder expressions of the acquisitive instinct; rather it is that these elements of a bustling civilization should be properly balanced with appropriate manifestations of a uniform system of manners and morals. To this end it was proposed that religion, morality, and knowledge should be encouraged by the schools, the churches, and the literature of the West.[11]

The McGuffey texts therefore dealt with the basic skills of reading and spelling, but approached these subjects within the specific educational framework of morality and citizenship. Furthermore, the basic skills to be developed and the character traits emphasized in the readers were not directly intended to develop among children a deep respect for the love of letters or the pursuit of philosophical issues, but rather to help instill in them basic literacy skills and the "correct" values necessary to enter into and succeed in industrializing America.

In the McGuffey readers, such issues as the accumulation and distribution of wealth were dealt with by accepting the inevitability of inequality, and that individual success, or lack of it, was a function of the morality and industriousness of the individual. Invariably, able-bodied men and women in the readers who appeared either as poor or criminal were depicted as either lazy, deceitful, alcoholic, or some combination of the three. Values presented as admirable in the McGuffey readers and by classroom teachers had to do with respect for authority, positive attitudes toward work, the value of thrift and savings, punctuality, and respect for the rights of others. Furthermore, by the 1870s and 1880s, both educators and business leaders began to claim that character training was the primary ingredient in individual success. In point of fact, it was frequently claimed, rural and/or poor students had the best potential for advancement in the United States, because growing up and having to adjust to adverse living conditions early in life was the best preparation for later competition in the business world.

Within this larger framework, both the children of the poor and the children of the rich needed to draw somewhat divergent messages from the stories and homilies presented in the readers: Frugality, industriousness, respectfulness, patience, truthfulness, and happiness were to be learned by all. Children of the well-to-do and/or those who later became successful in the adult world had the additional responsibility of recognizing the civic and moral obligation of success: that of voluntarily sharing or returning to society some measure of their wealth through philanthropic projects and/or charitable works. Meanwhile, for those finding themselves in more adverse conditions, admonitions to persevere were the norm:

Once or twice though you should fail,
    Try, Try Again;
If you would, at last, prevail,
    Try, Try Again;

If we strive, 'tis no disgrace,
 though we may not win the race;
What should you do in that case?
 Try, Try Again.
If you find your task is hard,
 Try, Try Again;
Time will bring you your reward,
 Try, Try Again;
All that other folks can do,
 Why with patience, should not you:
Only keep this rule in view;
 Try, Try Again.[12]

THE CITY BUILDING THEME LATE
IN THE NINETEENTH CENTURY

By the late nineteenth century, the argument that formal schooling could be instrumental in national development was no longer questioned by the American public. For example, many common school crusaders in the 1870s and 1880s argued that the American Civil War would never have been fought had "correct" moral and civic values been previously taught in the South. Because the South had been very slow to put public education into place, it was argued, Southerners had developed little respect for democracy and for character traits of honesty and fairness. Had such character traits been instilled in them, the war would never have happened. As well, many educators argued in the West that lingering "Indian problems" were basically educational problems. As soon as public education could be efficiently put into place on the reservations, the development of character traits necessary for transforming remaining groups of native Americans into decent, law-abiding citizens would follow.

 Educational issues in the rural South and West, however, were not the focus of most late nineteenth-century school reformers. As it was earlier in the century, continuing industrial expansion in America's cities was still the main interest of the period. The growth of business and transportation facilities within central cities had not only the effect of providing employment opportunities for many new workers, but also the negative impact of driving many middle-class people away from the noise and congestion of their former residential neighborhoods. As before, their places were more than filled by thousands upon thousands of immigrants and former citizens of the countryside (see Table 3.2). The net result of such developments was to further accelerate already serious urban demographic problems: people with few city-living skills, increasing numbers of non-Protestants and non-English-speaking people, and, in general, too many folks who displayed character traits offensive to the civic and moral values of middle-class

TABLE 3.2. IMMIGRANTS TO THE UNITED STATES:
1825–1925

Year	Number
1825	10,199
1835	45,374
1845	114,371
1855	200,877
1865	248,120
1875	227,498
1885	395,346
1895	258,536
1905	1,026,499
1915	326,700
1925	294,314

(Source: Data taken from Historical Statistics of the United States, Colonial Times to 1970 *[Washington, D.C.: U.S. Department of Commerce, Bureau of the Census], 1975, pp. 105–106.)*

fourth, fifth, and sixth generation Americans who had by now moved into outer areas of the city. According to Henry Perkinson, such conditions were viewed as a serious threat:

> Confronted with the deterioration of their cities, many native urban Americans placed the blame on the newcomers. The immigrants had produced the filth, the vermin, the diseases now found in the cities. The moral inadequacies of the newcomers had generated the slums that were now laying waste to urban life. Their great tendency to vagrancy and crime, their undemocratic backgrounds, and their lack of understanding of American institutions made them a menace to the city, if not to the nation itself. The newcomers were intemperate, illiterate and ignorant; they lived in filth and wallowed in corruption. But what was most frightening of all: they were breeding![13]

Increasing fear of the immigrants clearly suggests why the character-training focus of the common school had become vital by the late nineteenth century. And school reformers believed they had the solution to what they perceived as another important social problem: growing labor unrest in the large-scale industries of the day.

PUBLIC EDUCATION AND LABOR UNREST

Throughout the nineteenth century, rural America had rapidly given way to industrial America. Educators had argued that the civilizing effect of public schooling and character training was vitally necessary for a host of children upon whom future economic development would most assuredly depend. Feeling certain that the disputes and traditions of Europe would not trouble Americans, educators saw the future of the American dream as bright, assuming those from immigrant origins could be brought to appreciate the American republic and the qualities of character they would need to develop in order to further this dream.

However, not all social problems brought about by rapid industrialization and urbanization were related to starting a business and/or getting a job. For many, the most onerous problem of the emerging industrial order in America was the working conditions one experienced after gaining employment. As earlier writers like Marx had predicted, and as many socialists of the day were quick to point out, the contradictions of capitalism were quite apparent in the United States. It was not uncommon for workers to spend twelve to fourteen hours a day performing tedious work for low wages during this period. And, of course, there were no "safety net" programs like worker's compensation, unemployment benefits, disability insurance, or Social Security programs for those unable to earn a living.

Furthermore, the competition between growing companies was intense, and cost-cutting by owners of such companies was usually directed at the salaries of workers. One way to make production more efficient was to incorporate more and more machinery into manufacturing. In such a way, workers would become attendant to the machines and need fewer craft skills. And less highly qualified workers could then be hired at less expense.

Another cost-saving strategy, followed by many capitalists, was to employ children and women whenever possible, the logic being that they could be paid less and would not unionize as male workers had increasingly done throughout the century. In fact it wasn't until the next century that national child labor laws protected children from frequent exploitation by American industrialists. Organized labor was a prime mover behind various child labor regulations, thus helping to drive many children out of factories and into school enrollment at the same time.

The gap between workers and the unemployed in America was growing wider and more visible in the 1870s and 1880s. Some shrewd businessmen were able to reap vast fortunes virtually overnight, and frequently these fortunes were won by manipulating the stock market, rather than by productive ventures potentially benefiting the general public. Furthermore, even relatively underhanded techniques for getting rich quick were championed by corporate leaders, much to the dismay of those at the bottom of the economic order. Finally, contrary to the beliefs about progress and order being the outcome of American economic development, there were several severe recessions during the final decades of the nineteenth century. Such economic downturns had long been predicted by socialists in Europe, and the influence of socialist and anarchist thought in America began to flourish right around the turn of the century.

Predictably, and as was the case in other industrializing nations, criticisms of industrial practices in the United States were primarily to be found among the ranks of urban workers and the poor. Agricultural groups too began to develop collective organizations to lobby for policies more cognizant of their needs. In the cities, a strong labor movement grew during this period, and union strikes against big business were frequent, and sometimes violent. Educators, however, continued to believe either that poverty and unemployment were due to the poor attitudes and motives of workers and/or that problems in the workplace and the city were transitory and could be remedied through education. Strikes and walkouts against businesses, it was argued, were un-American and smacked of the foreign influence that those now running American institutions had worked against since early in the century. Merle Curti documented the pro-business and anti-labor attitudes of the educational establishment during this period:

> Hardly an annual meeting of the National Education Association was concluded without an appeal on the part of leading educators for the help of the teacher in quelling strikes and checking the spread of socialism and anarchism. Commissioners of education and editors of educational periodicals summoned their forces to the same end. Strikes were condemned as inexcusable attacks on the social order. In 1877 the president of the [NEA], in commenting on the railroad strikes, declared that the public school alone had saved the country from the terrors of the French Commune and that the outbreaks might have been entirely prevented had the workers been trained "to think as well as to toil."[14]

As this quotation clearly suggests, by the late nineteenth century the mission of the public school had become almost synonymous with advancing the cause of economic development. The role of the public school was to help the children of immigrants learn English, to teach all children basic literacy skills, to help them acquire the Protestant character traits necessary for them to be good workers, and to instill among all children a love for this country and its way of life. By the end of the century, however, many education and business leaders also began to suggest that the logic and desirability of capitalist economic development should become incorporated into the formal curriculum of the school. Character training would still remain important, but stronger ties between the needs of business and the purposes of public instruction needed to be forged. Significantly, references to the utility of the social sciences in advancing the cause of economic growth (the subject of our next two chapters) were first heard during this period.

> Although educators continued to develop more specifically the idea of moral training, as the period advanced they turned their attention increasingly to the social sciences as means by which schools might inculcate

respect for law and order, and suspicion for the doctrines of socialism and anarchism. As early as 1877 [the] superintendent of public instruction in Maryland declared that the elements of political economy, the nature and the relations of money, capital, labor, and wages, could be made as accessible to the young as the elements of grammar and arithmetic.[15]

SUMMARY

During the nineteenth century the American economy moved from being primarily rural and agriculturally based to one whose growing industries attracted many people from overseas, and from off the farm, into metropolitan areas. As economic and demographic changes occurred in the United States, the small and rural schools of the countryside were no longer seen as adequate for the needs of urban and industrial life. The Protestant virtues of hard work and respect for authority, coupled with the virtues of democratic civic life, needed to be taught to children. However, advocates of public educational systems in America's cities claimed that such values as political and basic literacy skills needed a new institutional framework.

The role of educators in facilitating economic development lay in helping to resolve several social problems brought about by industrialization. On the one hand, the lack of adequate supervision and character training necessary for entrance into the labor market called for educators equipped to aid in the moral development of immigrant and/or previously rural children. In addition, helping to rekindle a sense of civic responsibility among all citizens during a period of desirable yet rapid social change seemed a pressing concern. Importantly, the vast majority of educators, as well as people in business and industry, had increasingly come to equate advances in economic development with advances in the quality of individual and social life.

Then, as now, the condition of many poor city dwellers and many unhappy industrial workers in America was believed to be a function of their educational inadequacies. Unlike today, however, it was argued that citizen unrest was more typically due to poor moral and work habits, rather than to lack of skills. In order to "save" the children of discontented, misguided, and/or uninterested parents, the role of the public school ought to be further expanded. Most business leaders and increasing numbers of educators now believed the cause of public education was synonymous with the cause of economic growth. Thus, despite resistance from some labor organizations and various parent groups, the groundwork was well laid for subsequent educational policies linking the growing and changing needs of the economy with public education.

NOTES

1. Henry Perkinson, *The Imperfect Panacea: American Faith in Education, 1865–1976* (2nd. ed.). New York: Random House, 1977, pp. 3–4.
2. David Tyack and Elizabeth Hansot, *Managers of Virtue: Public School Leadership in America, 1820–1980.* New York: Basic Books, 1982.
3. Robert Mason, *Contemporary Educational Theory.* New York: David McKay, 1972, p. 25.
4. Carl Kaestle, *Pillars of the Republic: Common Schools and American Society, 1780–1860.* New York: Hill & Wang, 1983, pp. 6, 8–9.
5. *Ibid.,* pp. 25–26.
6. Henry Perkinson, *The Imperfect Panacea,* pp. 6–7.
7. Joel Spring, *The American School.* New York: Longman, 1986, p. 19.
8. Louis Fuller (ed.), Horace Mann, *On the Crisis in Education.* Yellow Springs, OH: The Antioch Press, 1965, pp. 88–91.
9. *Ibid.,* p. 131.
10. *Ibid.,* p. 124.
11. Richard Mosier, *Making the American Mind: Social and Moral Ideas in the McGuffey Readers.* New York: Russell and Russell, 1965, p. 158.
12. William McGuffey, *McGuffey's Newly Revised Eclectic Second Reader.* Cincinnati: Winthrop B. Smith, 1853, pp. 29–30.
13. Henry Perkinson, *The Imperfect Panacea,* p. 68.
14. Merle Curti, *The Social Ideas of American Educators,* Totowa, NJ: Littlefield, Adams, 1971, pp. 218–219.
15. *Ibid.,* p. 221.

FOR ADDITIONAL READING

There are a variety of histories of eighteenth- and nineteenth-century American education that attempt to deal with the impact of economic development on public instruction (and vice versa). Some of these are quoted in this text, and the interested reader should consult them. I would particularly recommend the works by Merle Curti, Henry Perkinson, Joel Spring, and David Tyack and Elizabeth Hansot for comprehensive histories of education during these centuries. The Kaestle work is also excellent, but deals more exclusively with pre-industrial America and its schools. Another favorite of mine (not cited on the previous page) is David Tyack's book *The One Best System* (Cambridge, MA: Harvard University Press, 1974).

Somewhat minimized in the previous account is a discussion of resistance (and alternatives) to the educational plans and policies of nineteenth-century educators and their assault on the "inferior" character traits of non-Protestant, poor, or working class children. Two interesting histories focusing on the middle class and Protestant bias of nineteenth-century school reformers and their allies are available in Michael Katz's *Irony of Early School Reform* (Cambridge, MA: Harvard University Press, 1968) and David Nasaw's *Schooled to Order* (New York: Oxford University Press, 1981). As both of these works suggest, a variety of groups and organizations then as now questioned the assertion that more economic growth would automatically alleviate poverty and inequality in America.

CHAPTER 4

Economics, Social Science, and Economic Development into the Twentieth Century

The story of economic development in the nineteenth century centered on the transformation of the United States from a primarily rural and small business economy into one of increasingly large manufacturing concerns located in increasingly urban and industrial settings. Similarly, the common school movement of the mid-nineteenth century primarily focused on the morals and character training deemed necessary for children to enter into and take advantage of this growing American economic system. The seeming success of economic growth in the United States was typically attributed to the hard work of the nation's citizens, and to the providence of God. Teaching America's children (especially immigrant children) the values and attitudes instrumental to full participation in the growing economy was a major theme in the rise and importance of public education.

By the late nineteenth century, however, a new and different rationale related both to continued economic growth and to issues in public schooling began to emerge. Specifically, calls for scientific understanding and the application of science to the needs of business and the needs of the school were increasingly heard during this period. Continuing in the pattern of Chapters 2 and 3, this chapter's emphasis will be on changing academic and intellectual notions about the process/dynamics of economic development in the late nineteenth century. In Chapter 5, we will discuss early twentieth-century educators as they attempted to further reform and extend public education for purposes of economic development, as guided by the "insights" of emerging social scientific and dominant business groups.

THE ECLIPSE OF POLITICAL ECONOMY

As we saw in Chapter 2, political economists of the late eighteenth and early nineteenth centuries were not only interested in wealth and economic productivity, but earnestly believed that the study of economics would lead to the discovery of the natural laws that governed economic processes. The more optimistic of the political economists believed that, once understood, natural economic laws could be put in the service of human betterment. However, during the past hundred years, most economists began to de-emphasize the moral and social concerns of political economy. John Stuart Mill is given much credit (or blame) for the observation that social laws were independent of economic laws, and that the proper study of economics ought to be differentiated from the study of social and philosophical issues.

At the same time, by the end of the nineteenth century, advances in data collection and mathematical manipulation of various income and production figures had made available to economists more scientific (i.e., quantifiable) analysis. Economists in the university typically viewed scientific rigor as both appropriate to their discipline, and a workable avenue to achieve status within the university community. According to Robert Heilbroner, economics by this period

> had ceased to be the proliferation of world views which now in the hands of a philosopher (Adam Smith), now a stockbroker (David Ricardo), now a revolutionary (Karl Marx) seemed to illuminate the whole avenue down which society was marching. It became instead the special province of professors whose investigations threw out pinpoint beams rather than the wide-searching beacons of the earlier economists. . . . economics [now] dealt with quantities and [anything] which dealt with quantities could be translated into mathematics. The process of translation required the abandonment of that tension-fraught world of the earlier economists, but it yielded in return a world of such neat precision and lovely exactness that the loss seemed amply compensated.[1]

The emerging mathematically minded economists who inherited the theories of earlier political economists began to write economics texts and publish primarily in economics journals, rather than in the older (and now perceived as value-laden) field of political economy. Thus, elaborately reasoned arguments behind the writings of political economists like Adam Smith concerning the nature of wealth and the benevolent consequences of unrestrained capitalism were increasingly accepted without much discussion by most of the new and more specialized economists. Economists who typically assumed the general validity and desirability of capitalist development by the late nineteenth century, and yet preferred mathematical assessments of economic production and consumption patterns over philosophical and social issues and debates of the day, are now typically known as neoclassical economists.

QUANTIFYING THE VALUE OF HUMAN RESOURCES

As mentioned in Chapter 2, a focal interest of all economists has been to understand and measure the value of manufactured goods. One dominant economic school of thought is that values are a function of the cost of physical capital, labor, and rent used in the manufacturing process. And with the mathematically rigorous standards becoming available to neoclassical economists, attempting to determine the value of goods through cost-of-production equations increased in popularity. Not surprisingly, some economists argued that humans were also produced, and the value of any human could therefore be mathematically determined. Therefore, some economists began to use this approach in quantifying the value of humans both to themselves and to their societies.

Pursuing a somewhat different line of inquiry, a few neoclassical economists around the turn of the twentieth century attempted to investigate more scientifically the value of aggregate human skills to national economic development, which Adam Smith and other political economists had suggested earlier. According to these economists, national costs of production and economic productivity calculations ought to take into account the variety of skills that workers had. Predicting and analyzing labor costs could be made more precise if mental and craft skills used in production were calculated as (human) capital, as opposed to physical labor. Among the nineteenth-century economists who made such arguments and attempted such measurements were Johann von Thunen, Leon Walras, and Irving Fisher.[2]

On the other hand, methodological efforts to differentiate worker skills and their utility in predicting economic growth were still rather rudimentary, given the types of data available on human skills. While attempts to statistically measure the value of human skills to national economies posed an interesting intellectual challenge to some economists, there seemed to be few direct policy implications arising from such research.

As was true earlier in the century, most skills were seen as learned on the job, and neoclassical economists still believed that the private sector ought to be left to its own devices. Also, the quandary first suggested by John Stuart Mill still remained: if economic development is supposed to be the avenue for advancing social progress, how can the skills of workers be separated from other qualities of people? That is, if people are to be the beneficiaries of economic development, should policy makers be in the business of helping manufacturers use people in this process? While each of the early human capital economists previously mentioned had partial answers to these questions, it would remain for mid-twentieth century economists, policy makers, and educators to propose economic development policies specifically linking government programs with the development of human capital. We will focus more particularly on this theme in Chapters 6 and 7.

INTERESTS AND PERSPECTIVES
AMONG EMERGING SOCIAL SCIENTISTS

The fact that most neoclassical economists were less interested in matters of political economy did not mean that all social and philosophical issues related to economic development were abandoned by academics. Instead, a new breed of social scientists began to emerge by the latter part of the century in the fields we now know as sociology, anthropology, and psychology. Furthermore, many questions regarding social dynamics in developing European countries were tackled head-on at the turn of the twentieth century by "transitional" scholars like Herbert Spencer, Emile Durkheim, Thorstein Veblen, and Max Weber. Such scholars were still very much interested in earlier discussions of political economy as it might be applied to understanding social rather than merely economic change. Yet their interests were increasingly seen as nonscientific by their peers in economics bent on more narrowly defined pursuits. In the case of each of these writers, interest in topics such as the nature and dynamics of social inequality, forces affecting social stability and social change, personality and family characteristics of individuals of different social classes, habits of occupationally "successful" and "unsuccessful" social groups, and processes of cultural change was central.

THE THEORY OF EVOLUTION
AND THE RISE OF SOCIAL SCIENCE

In England, the period between 1850 and 1890 had been economically productive and relatively progressive compared to the social dislocation, poverty, and warfare that raged throughout Europe during the previous century. Predictably, business leaders and neoclassical economists alike proclaimed that social progress in England, and later in the rest of Europe, was due to the wonderful world that unrestrained capitalism had brought about. Thus, the evolution of capitalism was increasingly viewed as synonymous with the social and cultural progress of humanity. The social sciences began to undertake studies of these processes.

During the late nineteenth century the concept of evolution had come into prominence due to the work of Charles Darwin. Darwin had convincingly argued that biological species evolved to adapt productively to changes in their environment. The process of natural selection occurred in such a fashion that genetic mutations occurring among species which facilitated their adaption to changing physical environments would be reproduced among successive generations, while those mutations dysfunctional to adaptability would lead to the eventual extinction of those carrying inappropriate genetic material.

Herbert Spencer was one of several early social scientists who reasoned that, if biological organisms evolved in such a fashion, so too might cultural systems. He argued that Victorian England (and later the United States) with its evolving economic and political system was the highest form of cultural adaptation humans faced within their physical environments. Given such a belief, both theoretical and policy questions emerged. The theoretical task for Spencer (and numerous others) lay in developing a model for placing cultures on some continuum from most primitive to most modern; several typologies were presented by such scholars during this time.

In addition, Spencer and a number of other "social Darwinists" also believed that their new insights into the evolution of cultures had important policy implications for government leaders and philanthropic organizations. Specifically, they felt that since economic development paved the way for cultural evolution, government or citizen efforts to interfere with capitalist development would in the long run harm society. Laws that blocked the cultural evolution of capitalism in the name of workers' rights or environmental protection, Spencer argued, impeded the natural order of progress and therefore should be resisted. Furthermore, Spencer believed that future cultural evolution of capitalist countries would depend on acknowledging and rewarding those members of society most important in stimulating economic and cultural growth, while those at the bottom of society should be discouraged from breeding and passing along the inferior genes that were responsible for their poverty and frequent criminal behavior.

As such a theory clearly suggests, Spencer was articulating and elaborating on several notions of earlier political economists, although his arguments were made under the scientific rubric of sociology rather than that of political economy. For example, his argument about the desirability of allowing the economic system to operate freely and without state intervention was very similiar to that of Adam Smith. And his analysis of the problem of the poor was in many ways very similiar to the lament of Thomas Malthus. Clearly, however, Spencer's reasoning was not consistent with that of John Stuart Mill, who had earlier declared that economic development was to benefit human social development, rather than be subject to it (nor, obviously, to the interpretations of Robert Owen or Karl Marx).

STRUCTURAL-FUNCTIONAL SOCIOLOGY

A French sociologist, Emile Durkheim, likewise grappled with social questions that were once the province of earlier political economists. Like Spencer, Durkheim was interested in delineating and elaborating on what it was the field of sociology ought to investigate, and the correct empirical methods human sciences ought to use in doing so. Like Spencer, Durkheim reasoned that the evolution of capitalism had a great potential for enhancing the human condition. However, he disagreed with the social Darwinists that social evolution followed naturally from economic evolution. Rather, Durkheim believed that while economic development could lead to social progress, the changes in social structure necessary for this to occur were problematic. Significantly, Durkheim argued that social scientific methods needed to be utilized in understanding the social dynamics of economic change.

A major substantive question for Durkheim, and one very central to the thought of earlier political economists, was the nature of social stability during the incredible economic and demographic changes in Western nations during the nineteenth and early twentieth centuries. Durkheim reasoned that laws of the community and those of social groups in which people lived out their lives gave frames of personal reference that all individuals needed in order to survive and prosper. But with the breakdown of cottage industries under capitalism, rapid specialization and division of labor among industrial workers, the decline of religion in an increasingly secular world, and the realignment of many political states during this period, Durkheim worried that normlessness (or anomie) would occur and potentially jeopardize economic and social progress. In other words, essential social functions (like socialization) earlier provided by the family and the church would need new structures in the modern world. Thus, Durkheim foresaw the need for integrating social institutions whose function would be to help humans adjust to the new national and international economic communities on the horizon. Durkheim argued that sociologists could play a vital role in helping to develop these new institutions.

Durkheim therefore partially agreed with Mill's pronouncement that the "natural laws" of economics could prescribe no social policies related to capitalist development. However, Durkheim felt that social science could. Specifically, he argued that the natural laws of society demanded group cohesion among societies' members and could not be taken for granted during times of rapid social change such as the industrializing Europe of his day. As you may have guessed, Durkheim stood strongly for the establishment and enhancement of public education. In order for society to remain coherent for individuals, and for desirable specialization and division of labor to proceed within an evolving capitalist economy, the state needed to intervene in the lives of children by helping to socialize them into what otherwise would appear as confusing, incoherent, and normless social environments. Most importantly, Durkheim declared that social stability and a shared sense of purpose were natural laws necessary for social progress and that such social prerequisites were guaranteed neither by God nor by the laws of economics. Agreeing with American educators like Horace Mann, then, Durkheim argued that although character training was important, such training was not a moral necessity, but rather a social/structural one. According to Durkheim:

. . . every society sets up a certain ideal of man, of what he should be, as much from the intellectual point of view as the physical and moral. This ideal is, in some degree, the same for all members of society; but it also becomes differentiated beyond a certain point, according to the specific groupings that every society contains in its structure. It is this ideal, which is both integral and diverse, that is the focus of education. . . . Education is the influence exercised by adult generations on those that are not yet ready for social life. Its object is to stimulate and develop in the child a certain number of physical, intellectual and moral states which are demanded of him by both the political society as a whole, and by the particular milieu for which he is specifically destined. . . .[3]

APPLYING SOCIAL SCIENCE
TO PROCESSES OF PRODUCTION

In addition to the more general theories of the social Darwinists (like Spencer) and functionalists (like Durkheim), there were also some social scientists very interested in how to apply social science directly to the production process. That is, making the capitalist workplace more efficient through careful analysis of the workplace and the actual processes required of workers in production became of keen interest to applied social scientists like Frederick Taylor. As you may recall, classical economists like Adam Smith had talked of the inevitability and desirability of the division of labor, and later sociologists like Durkheim theorized that such a process would continue to develop as time progressed. With the division of the manufacture of goods (Adam Smith was fascinated with pin production) into subspecialties, different workers could be hired at different wages for different jobs, thus producing more goods at less cost.

According to efficiency experts like Taylor, such a general theory was all well and good, and perhaps had intuitively guided much of capitalism since its inception; however, late nineteenth-century science could help streamline and even accelerate this process by specifically analyzing the workplace and the movements of workers. With this knowledge, workrooms and shop floors could be rearranged to minimize inefficient traffic flows. By carefully matching the required movements for particular jobs to the physical competencies of specific workers, the hiring and job training of occupational specialists could be scientifically pursued, thus enhancing worker output and owner profit.

Such a line of reasoning, ostensibly guided by the insight of both the physical and social sciences, gave rise to the school of scientific management and further enhanced the status of science in the business world. Not coincidentally, Taylor also argued that business proficiency demanded the separation of management from the actual production process. Workers, claimed Taylor, had neither the time nor the interest in advancing the cause of efficient management in production, because they tended to be more concerned with peer relationships and/or craftsmanship. However, efficiency and precision in production were central to both the interests of management science and the profit motives of employers—a good example, argued the scientific management specialists, of how science can help to further the legitimate aims of capitalists and the larger economic development interests of the United States. According to Harry Braverman:

> Taylor created a simple line of reasoning and advanced it with a logic and clarity, a naive openness, and an evangelical zeal which soon won him a strong following among capitalists and managers. His work began in the 1880s but it was not until the 1890s that he began to lecture, read papers, and publish results. . . . The essential element[s of Taylor's insight are] the systematic pre-planning and pre-calculation of all elements of the labor process, which now no longer exist as a process in the imagination of the worker but only as a process in the imagination of a special management staff. Thus if the first principle is the gathering and development of knowledge of labor processes, and the second is the concentration of this knowledge as the exclusive province of management, [then] the third is the use of this monopoly over knowledge to control each step of the labor process and its mode of execution.[4]

EARLY CONFLICT THEORIES IN SOCIAL SCIENCE

For the most part, early sociologists and anthropologists believed that economic development and social development were desirable and interrelated. As the case of Emile Durkheim clearly illustrates, however, many such social scientists also believed that the natural laws of economics (now under the investigation of economists) were inadequate as models for discussing the social dynamics of economic progress. A common belief among them was that social science could aid in the process of economic development by clarifying the attitudes and beliefs necessary for such progress to occur and by helping to construct social institutions for such purposes.

On the other hand, other prominent social scientists like Max Weber and Thorstein Veblen argued that the increasingly accepted economic and social theories inspired by the supposed natural laws of economics or biological evolution were too simplistic or seriously flawed. Nor were many of them convinced about the scientific validity of historical materialism as offered by Karl Marx. As sociologists, both Weber and Veblen disagreed with the assumption of many classical and neoclassical economists that economic objectives (however rationally pursued) were the "building blocks" of human culture. Each instead argued that social groups channel and direct the creative and consumptive interests of individuals in society. Indeed, to assume that each group's short- or long-term interests were in accord with those of all other groups in society, or that "progress" was inevitable and/or necessarily desirable, was merely wishful (and nonscientific) thinking.

Thorstein Veblen was an economist who stood clearly outside what had already become mainstream economics in the early twentieth century. He was particularly intrigued with anthropological discoveries of the status and prestige rituals of "primitive" societies. Based on such discoveries, he argued that many significant cross-cultural events and customs could be explained more easily with reference to human "irrationalities" than in terms of rational behavior. Far too much emphasis on form, grace, styles of dress, manners of warfare, and rules of etiquette existed within almost every identified culture to ever be explained with reference to specifically economic activities. So too, modern capitalist nations like Britain and the United States contained entire social groups whose importance to continued economic development was virtually nil. And these groups were the very ones to which the social Darwinists like Spencer attributed all the economic success of Western culture!

> Veblen's central idea in regard to the modern capitalist world is that it is based on an irremediable opposition between business and industry, ownership and technology . . . between those who make goods and those who make money, between workmanship and salesmanship. . . . His fellow evolutionists [e.g., Herbert Spencer] argued that the leading industrialists and men of finance, having shown in the competitive struggle that they were "the fittest," had to be regarded as the flowers of modern civilization. Veblen argued that, far from being the fittest agents of evolutionary advancement, men engaged in pecuniary activities were parasites growing fat on the technological leadership and innovation of other men.[5]

For Veblen, the harbingers of future economic and social development in Western culture were the technicians and engineers generated by the science of technology and its applications to human problems. Furthermore, the beauty of technological advance and mechanization in the workplace was that the rational processes needed in production had the potential of altering much of the (typically dangerous) irrational behavior of individuals and social groups outside of the workplace. Furthermore, economic and social progress could best be facilitated by limiting or removing capitalist control over economic development, because such individuals were not interested in the solving of social or economic problems per se, but rather in lining their own pockets through manipulating the needs of consumers and/or lending them the money to buy things they didn't really need in the first place.

For Max Weber, too, the assumption that individual and rational consumer choices determined the direction of economic growth and development needed to be investigated rather than tacitly accepted by those attempting to explain the phenomenal changes in Western cultures since the seventeenth century. Specifically, in *The Protestant Ethic and the Spirit of Capitalism,* Weber declared that capitalism as an economic force emerged in eighteenth-century Europe not because of the rational goal-related choices of individuals, but because of the Protestant ethos (primarily Calvinist) that emerged there in the centuries just before capitalism "took off."

In essence, Weber argued that Protestant concern with going to heaven after death led to the hard work and capital accumulation on which economic development depended for its success. Since conspicuous consumption of material goods or displays of wealth were viewed as sinful, and since only through hard work and competition could believers be rewarded in the afterlife, such groups in essence introduced the rationality, energy, and business practices that allowed capitalism to take hold. According to Weber, this effect on the capitalist system was unintentional; it was not primarily caused by the rational choices made by consumers. Rather, it was a natural by-product of the moral and ethical preoccupations of Protestantism.

As opposed to both Spencer and Durkheim (and Veblen), Weber viewed capitalism and the bureaucratic rationality that went with it as, at best, a mixed blessing. Instead of bringing about a new utopian existence for humankind, industrial capitalism primarily caused the emergence of a different status system, complete with new rationalities and contradictions. Instead of freeing human capabilities and intellect, it provided yet new ways and means for constraining human potential.

> Weber [identified] bureaucracy with rationality, and the process of rationalization with mechanism, depersonalization, and oppressive routine. Rationality, in this context, [was] seen as adverse to personal freedom. . . . [and] he deplore[d] the type of man that the mechanization and the routine of bureaucracy selects and forms.[6]

Finally, Weber agreed with other conflict theorists like Veblen (and to a great extent, Marx) that a person's location within the economic system (i.e., one's economic class) had a powerful effect on his or her beliefs, culture, and consumption patterns. However, Weber also argued that religion, occupation, geography, gender, and ethnic background had an important effect on the way members of such associational groups interpreted reality; these factors influenced their behavior in many respects.

> In Weber's view every society is divided into groupings and strata with distinctive life-styles and views of the world, just as it is divided into distinctive classes. While at times status as well as class groupings may

conflict, at others their members may accept fairly stable patterns of subordination. . . . With this twofold classification of social stratification, Weber lays the groundwork for an understanding of pluralistic forms of social conflict in modern society and helps to explain why only in rare cases are such societies polarized into opposing camps of "haves" and "have-nots." He has done much to explain why Marx's exclusively class-centered scheme failed to predict correctly the shape of things to come in modern pluralistic societies.[7]

As this quotation suggests, Weber disagreed also with Veblen's hope for a society guided by technicians and engineers. Such groups, he argued, would seek out privileged status for themselves and evaluate other groups as inferior along the dimensions of technological rationality, which would undergird their associational cultures.

NEO-MARXIST CONSTRUCTS FOR INTERPRETING CAPITALIST POLITICAL ECONOMY

For Marx and his followers, the acceptance by economists and functionalist social scientists of the inevitability and/or desirability of capitalism did not weaken the tenets of earlier classical political economy, but rather demonstrated that what was once debatable was now part of the ideology of Western culture. Thus, analysis and scholarship within the Marxian community has continually sought to investigate and articulate how the political economy of capitalist economic growth and development has infiltrated into every sphere of consciousness and social policy in capitalist nations.

According to Marxist theory, the evolution of capitalism would bring about several extreme contradictions that would threaten its continued existence. One of these contradictions focused on the long-term possibilities of a market system that depended on workers and owners as consumers. According to Marxist theory, workers would earn less and less in the future as market forces caused capitalists to continually decrease their wages in order to compete with other capitalists. Thus, instead of being able to continually purchase the fruits of economic production, in the advanced stages of capitalism the working class would have to spend more and more of their dwindling income on food rather than manufactured goods. In turn, those at the top of the economic order would at some point reach a point of satiation, where they would in essence have everything they wanted. At such a point, the economy would have to come to a standstill, because consumer goods would no longer be purchased by anyone. According to Marx, when both classes either could not or would not purchase any more manufactured goods, the economy would stagnate. With a stagnant economy, workers would have to be laid off. And when everyone was finally unemployed, it would appear obvious to all that the reason for unemployment was that the profit motive of capitalists was responsible for the ruined economy and society.

However, the collapse of capitalism in the most advanced Western nations did not occur. If anything, according to most nineteenth-century social historians, things were getting better and better in the already industrialized nations. Not only was the economic standard of living increasing in the West during this period, but so too were the political and social entitlements of its citizens by the end of the nineteenth century. Part of the answer to how society might reconcile the potentially adverse conditions of capitalism had been suggested by Mills, and in fact much social legislation was directed at addressing excesses of liberal capitalism. The state, according to Karl Polanyi, became an important arena for occupational and social groups not in control of industrial development:

> By the turn of the nineteenth century . . . the working class was an influential factor in the state; the trading classes, on the other hand, whose sway over the legislature was no longer unchallenged, became conscious of the political power involved in their leadership in industry. This peculiar localization of influence and power caused no trouble as long as the market system continued to function without great stress and strain; but when, for inherent reasons, this was no longer the case, and when tensions between the social classes developed, society itself was endangered by the fact that the contending parties were making government and business, state and industry, respectively, their strongholds.[8]

If the end of capitalism was not in sight, and if economic growth and social progress were continuing to occur simultaneously in England and the rest of Europe, there had to be some underlying reason. According to several radical economists, the key to understanding how and why economic growth remained positive in Europe lay in understanding the nature of colonialism as practiced among the Western nations from the mid-nineteenth to the mid-twentieth centuries. By late in the nineteenth century,

> The age of imperialism had begun, and the map makers were changing the colors which denoted the ownership of the darker continents. Between 1870 and 1898 Britain added 4 million square miles and 88 million people to its empire; France gained nearly the same area of territory with 40 million souls attached; Germany won a million miles and 30 million people; even Portugal joined the race with 800,000 miles of new lands and 9 million inhabitants. . . . And then, too, the process of empire building brought with it prosperity for the empire builders. No small part of the gain in working-class conditions . . . was the result of sweated labor overseas: the colonies were now the proletariat's proletariat. No wonder imperialism was a popular policy.[9]

Conveniently, argued radical scholars, Western political leaders and functionalist social scientists believed that subjugating African and Asian nations of the world to the supposed superiority of Western culture primarily benefited these peoples. In fact, neo-Marxists argued, such ethnocentric thinking was merely masking the oppression and violence being done to those cultures, while at the same time benefiting the development of markets and sources of raw materials for developing Western economies. Such confusion, obviously to the benefit of capitalists in each of the colonial empires, was increasingly being incorporated into the popular ideology of Western nations:

> A new and vigorous spirit was sweeping England and the Continent and even the United States, a spirit which manifested itself in the proliferation of such slogans as "The Anglo-Saxon race is infallibly destined to be the predominant force in the history and civilization of the world."[10]

Thus, socialist thinkers undertook to redefine the evolution of capitalist economic development to include international capitalism, of which imperialism represented to them a new and final stage. At home, this smug belief in the beneficence of western culture would continue to affect commonsense notions about the desirability and inevitability of capitalist development; internationally it would lead to war.

SUMMARY

By the end of the nineteenth century, economic development in the Western world was well advanced. During this period, the field of economics had become a legitimate scientific enterprise and had increasingly begun to analyze and concentrate on dynamics of production and trade within the private sector. At the same time, most neoclassical economists made assumptions about the rational and goal-related behavior of humans and became less interested in many of the moral and philosophical questions of earlier political economists. By and large, economists of the late nineteenth century believed that economic development would proceed logically and efficiently without government interference or control.

Meanwhile, the social problems and opportunities associated with economic development became the focus of the new academic fields of sociology, anthropology, and psychology. Some social scientists, like the social Darwinists, found the process of economic development among Western nations benign and progressive. They typically agreed with neoclassical economists that economic development was good, because such development was related to cultural evolution as well as the satisfaction of individual consumption preferences.

Other sociologists and anthropologists believed that economic development was positive, yet foresaw that social problems were possible within societies facing rapid social change. Such scholars argued that a true science of society was possible and that such a science could inform government policy for the potential enhancement of cultural evolution. Emile Durkheim, for example, argued that public schooling for young children would be a good social investment for a developing country, as older processes of bringing children into rapidly changing cultures might break down in the process of social change. Still a few others, like Frederick Taylor, believed that a science of the division of labor necessary to advance the cause of economic development was possible and useful, primarily in the private sector.

On the other hand, a few economists and social scientists wrote in the late nineteenth century about the conflict of interest that they believed best described social dynamics under capitalist economic development. Some viewed the emerging social order not as the backdrop for new liberating social relationships among all people, but rather as a new arena for status and class distinctions. Furthermore, some argued that human insecurities and vanities, rather than true human needs, supplied the motivation of consumers and producers. Because humans were basically irrational, unnecessary products flooded the market frequently, making those who catered to human foibles rich, compared to those who might truly be contributing to human progress.

Furthermore, Marxist critics had a different interpretation about why European nations appeared to be doing so well economically. In essence, their claim was that much of the cost of production involved in economic development was being subsidized by colonies of the West. In particular, many of the raw materials and much of the labor used to produce wealth in Europe was coming from colonies of the European nations. By converting these traditional societies into economic satellites of the mother countries, Western nations were able to raise standards of living at home, while virtually ruining traditional ways of life in their colonies. Furthermore, in efforts to maintain and enhance standards of living in Europe (and the U.S.), the economically developed nations would continue to seek domination over "backward" nations for further purposes of exploitation. And such a dynamic would lead not to ever expanding and peaceful economic development, but to continual exploitation and war.

With regard to the concept of education and the process of economic development, most economists and social scientists had little to say. Durkheim, for example, felt as did Horace Mann that schooling for young children would be socially important in rapidly changing societies to help build social cohesion. However, he also argued that particular trade skills ought to be taught in the private sector and/or learned in apprenticeship. And given the newness of their sciences, most other interested scholars were still concerned more with description and theory than with prescribing how governments ought to become involved, if at all, in the economic development process. This would all change soon.

NOTES

1. Robert Heilbroner, *The Worldly Philosophers*. New York: Simon & Schuster, 1967, pp. 156–157.
2. B. F. Kiker, "The Historical Roots of the Concept of Human Capital," *Journal of Political Economy,* 74 (5), 1966: 481–499.
3. Emile Durkheim, "Education and Sociology," in Anthony Giddens (ed.), *Emile Durkheim: Selected Writings.* Cambridge; Cambridge University Press, 1972, pp. 203–204.
4. Harry Braverman, *Labor and Monopoly Capital: The Degradation of Work in the Twentieth Century.* New York: Monthly Review Press, 1974, pp. 91, 119.
5. Lewis Coser, *Masters of Sociological Thought.* New York: Harcourt Brace Janovich, 1971, p. 266.
6. H. Gerth and C. Wright Mills, *From Max Weber: Essays in Sociology.* New York: Oxford University Press, 1946, p. 50.
7. Coser, *Masters of Sociological Thought,* pp. 229–230.
8. Karl Polanyi, *The Great Transformation.* Boston: Beacon Press, 1944, p. 133.
9. Heilbroner, *Worldly Philosophers,* pp. 174–175.
10. *Ibid.,* p. 173.

FOR ADDITIONAL READING

Several original writings by late nineteenth- and early twentieth-century social scientists are worth reading with regard to social change and economic development. Among them are Emile Durkheim's work *The Division of Labor in Society* (New York: Free Press, 1964), and his educational perspective as offered in *Education and Society* (New York: Free Press, 1973). Herbert Spencer's sociological analysis is best outlined in his *Principles of Sociology* (New York: Appleton, 1884), while the competing interpretation of the possible use of sociology for improving the human condition is available in Lester Frank Ward's *Dynamic Sociology* (New York: Appleton, 1883).

More critical appraisals of the social possibilities of economic development are provided by Thorstein Veblen in *The Theory of the Leisure Class* (New York: Modern Library, 1934), and by Max Weber. Perhaps the best annotated collection of Weber's work is contained in the volume edited by H. Gerth and C. Wright Mills entitled *From Max Weber: Essays in Sociology* (New York: Oxford University Press, 1946).

Good secondary sources for most of the social science perspectives presented in this chapter are Lewis Coser's *Masters of Sociological Thought* (New York: Harcourt Brace Janovich, 1971) and Randall Collin's *Three Sociological Traditions* (New York: Oxford University Press, 1985). The Marxist interpretation of the dynamics of the division of labor under capitalism is eloquently presented by Harry Braverman in *Labor and Monopoly Capital: The Degradation of Work in the Twentieth Century* (New York: Monthly Review Press, 1974). In addition, the general decline of interest among economists in moral philosophy or other topics of political economy is discussed at more length by Robert Heilbroner in *The Worldly Philosophers* (New York: Simon & Schuster, 1967).

CHAPTER 5

The Transition to
the Twentieth Century:
Social Science, Education,
and Economic Development

As various educators and academics who appeared in Chapters 3 and 4 pointed out, individual morality in America (and in the other industrialized nations) had become closely associated during the nineteenth century with occupational success. The economic development of the nation was typically argued to be a function of the (Protestant) Christian virtues of hard work, thrift, investment, and clean living exhibited by its people. The role of the common school, then, was to be an institutionally organized setting for the masses. In such institutions, it was argued, the character traits believed necessary for individual and national economic growth could be developed among all children, and particularly among those who might otherwise fall by the wayside. Importantly, most small businessmen, teachers, school administrators, and academics all claimed the moral bases of both their private and their professional lives came from their Protestant religious beliefs and aspirations.

By the turn of the twentieth century, however, the application of Protestant Christian morality so important in justifying early school reform began to be abandoned and/or altered by the academic, business, and educational communities. Most academics in both the physical and social sciences had begun to argue that there was order in the universe that was predictable and understandable. Biological organisms and social organisms were not divine mysteries, and their workings could be investigated and analyzed through scientific investigation. According to scientists, the evolution of species and of cultures could be understood (and some said, controlled).

In many ways, leaders in the private sector concurred with the academics. While morality and godliness were still desirable traits for individuals, the success of large-scale business organizations and international trade activities for our national economy would call for better planning, management, and coordination skills than religious leaders could provide. Increasingly, such needs were seen to require the perspectives and advice of economists, political leaders and applied social scientists. And from the late nineteenth century onward, many social scientists and economists were quite willing to share their perspectives and give their advice to receptive business groups in the U.S.

DEBATES OVER THE FORM AND SUBSTANCE OF SECONDARY SCHOOLING

Debates over the form and function of public education by the end of the century primarily centered on secondary education. As was discussed previously, explicit skills training for occupational success received little emphasis in the common (now elementary) school. Its manifest purpose was to instill the character traits and values (along with English instruction for immigrants) argued to be prerequisites of individual entrepreneurship and sound Christian living.

However, as industrialists then and historians now have argued, employment patterns by the end of the nineteenth century clearly favored large-scale organizations as opposed to the proliferation of small businesses that common school advocates attempted to educate children for earlier in the century. The very limited secondary schooling opportunities of the mid-nineteenth century were primarily geared to college preparation, not occupational training. By late in the century, however, secondary school enrollments had begun to increase rapidly. According to the educational historian C.H. Edson:

> The growth of public secondary education around the turn of the century was phenomenal by any standard. Between 1890 and 1920 new high schools opened on the average of over one per day, and student enrollments increased by 812 percent compared with a nationwide population increase during the same period of only 68 percent. Most important, however, were figures reflecting the percentage of youth, ages fourteen to seventeen, enrolled in public schools: from 4 percent in 1890, the figures swelled to 28 percent by 1920, and to 47 percent by 1930.[1]

Increasing demand for education beyond common schooling seemed to be the result of several economic and social factors. Lack of employment opportunities for some youth due to late nineteenth-century economic recessions was one of these. Another seemed to have been the perceived importance of higher education for the social advancement aspired to by the emerging middle class in America's cities. Various labor organizations also appeared to believe that public schools might be a good avenue for working class children to gain skills and perspectives not available in entry level (and increasingly "deskilled") positions in the workforce. Institutions of higher learning were typically on the lookout for new students, and a fresh supply of youngsters with more than basic literacy skills might help colleges and universities expand in the future.

Naturally, most of these groups were interested in different curricular opportunities for their children. And each of them made good cases for why all Americans would benefit from public taxes to support secondary education. Strong support for extending the liberal arts education model was advanced by higher education spokespersons like William Torrey Harris. He argued that the increasing demand for education among the public was a function of our successful economic development, and that finally the pursuit of knowledge and higher order thinking skills might rightfully be available to all citizens interested in pursuing them. This line of argument pleased not only many higher education advocates, but also the parents of the growing number of middle- and working-class children with aspirations of enlightenment and social advancement for their children. Many of these, no doubt, had taken to heart the possibilities of social uplift earlier espoused by advocates of common schooling (like Horace Mann).

On the other hand, American social Darwinists like William Graham Sumner, a student of Herbert Spencer, saw little economic or social utility for public education beyond grade school. Both Spencer and Sumner believed that the teaching of science and the scientific method (as opposed to Christian morality) should be taught to individuals, but that such instruction was best performed by private schools and colleges rather than by the state. If education was something worth having, then it should be subject to the laws of supply and demand, and not be something provided by the government. Also, since the social Darwinists doubted whether the average citizen had the talent for understanding complex academic material, attempting to teach advanced concepts to incapable students would be a great waste of public monies. In general, both Spencer and Sumner argued that state-sponsored education had a tendency to promote ameliorist or equality-of-opportunity schemes. And such schemes, they contended, merely postponed or delayed social progress.

In evaluating the educational contributions of the American sociologist Sumner, historian Lawrence Cremin insists that he "maintained a healthy bias against public education in general," and that:

> while he supported limited compulsory education, he believed in it more as a guarantee of public order than a lever of social uplift. He inveighed unceasingly against pedagogical faddists of every sort and variety, assum-

ing that most proposals for reform were nostrums designed to avoid the irksome labor essential to true mental discipline. And he was equally caustic in his criticism of all public plans for popularizing knowledge among the masses. Ultimately he placed his faith in the processes of nature. The principal contribution of sociology, he concluded, would be to awaken men to the enormous complexity of the social organism, and hence to the slim prospects for the rapid alleviation of social problems.[2]

INDUSTRIAL EDUCATION: ATTEMPTS TO COUPLE PUBLIC DEMAND FOR EDUCATION WITH NEEDS OF THE PRIVATE SECTOR

By the turn of the twentieth century, the facts were these: there was a growing demand for education beyond common schooling; there were competing arguments about what this education should look like; and while new schools went up daily in many cities, there continued to be dissension among taxpayers within such cities regarding how much, if any, they ought to pay for secondary education. The more reluctant of these citizens typically resisted notions that they should write a blank check for schools in which they had no children; they could not understand how they or the rest of the public would benefit from them.

Business organizations had become powerful forces within city government circles; they also seemed unwilling to help underwrite public education programs favoring curricular initiatives unrelated to the needs of business and industry. Worse, they feared that the radical viewpoints of organized labor might be presented in secondary school classrooms. Furthermore, according to many businessmen, the role of city, state, and federal governments was not to interfere more than necessary with the process of economic development. After all, they claimed, the United States was by this time the leading export nation in the world. Yet, in order to remain economically competitive, more investment in the private sector was needed, not taxes on business profits for the sake of a few students trying to escape the world of work by becoming "intellectuals." Of course, such a line of reasoning was also the conventional wisdom among neoclassical economists.

However, there were at least three interrelated problems with the labor needs of business that an expanding public education sector might address, according to some business groups. Given the increasing division of labor in America's growing factories, the very specific skills new workers needed for occupational placement had few viable training programs. Furthermore, since older workers still clung to notions of craftsmanship, rather than to an emerging rationale of efficiency (as espoused by applied social scientists like Taylor), apprenticeship systems run by craft unions were seen as outdated and inefficient. Finally, the emerging industrial order called for commitments to the company and its profit-oriented needs rather than to individual entrepreneurship or craftsmanship. Somehow, entering workers needed to be "educated" as to how they stood in relation to the larger competitive needs of their employers and their nation, and to begin thinking beyond their personal or their own craft guild's interests.

In order then to take advantage of increasing public demand for education, while at the same time focusing the content of such education on their own emerging labor concerns, several organized business groups helped to sponsor and lead the Industrial Education movement of the early twentieth century. Furthermore, proponents of Industrial Education already had an international secondary school model to which they could refer, as well as some consulting economists who could argue that the long-standing interest in the value of human capital had policy implications for economic development interests of the nation. Germany, Industrial Education supporters argued, had already publicly financed secondary programs for industrial education, and the economist Irving Fischer had documented that worker skills were an important component of U.S. national wealth.

One of the primary supporters of the Industrial Education Movement was the powerful National Association of Manufacturers (NAM). An important NAM "crusade" was to convince national, state, and local leaders about what they perceived as the necessity for linking the emerging specialized needs of industry with the growing public education system.

According to "reports" sponsored by the National Association of Manufacturers, the right to earn a wage and be gainfully employed was one of the most important "opportunities" guaranteed by American democracy. Yet, while even such "undemocratic" nations as Germany had recognized the need to integrate industrial and trade education into their educational system, Americans were being denied such opportunities in the twentieth century, and our industries were losing the battle of competitiveness in the process. According to NAM, labor unions were primarily responsible for denying and delaying the adoption of more and better industrial education programs in our secondary schools. Labor groups such as the American Federation of Labor had declared that turning out too many workers for specific trades would lead to overspecialization and/or underemployment. To the contrary, argued the NAM, increasing the pool of qualified workers would enhance equality of opportunity, individual autonomy, and national competitiveness. According to NAM's Committee on Industrial Education in 1905:

> The absurd doctrine that we as a nation can have too many skilled mechanics or that the American youth can be too well educated in his trade or calling, is as we say, unaccountable. It ought to be recognized as a scientific truth that the higher the skill possessed by a mechanic the more

valuable is his labor, both to himself and to his employer and the community. . . . technical and trade education for youth is a national necessity, and [the] nation that wins success in competition with other nations must train its youth in the arts of production and distribution. . . . [Meanwhile] the German technical and trade schools are at once the admiration and fear of all countries. In the world's race for commercial supremacy, we must copy and improve upon the German method of education. Germany relies chiefly upon her trained workers for her commercial success and prosperity. She puts no limit on the money to be expended in trade and technical education.[3]

Seven years later, the NAM-sponsored Committee on Industrial Education went even further in justifying why most secondary education ought to be preparatory for occupational placement. In their report of 1912, the concept of human capital was for one of the first times specifically used to substantiate educational policy proposals in the United States:

There are two kinds of capital in the world. The one we call property. It consists of lands and machinery, of stocks and bonds, etc. This kind of capital we are abundantly developing. The other kind is human capital— the character, brains and muscle of the people. Professor Fischer, of Yale, at the head of a very able committee, estimates the human capital, the human resources of our country, as of the money value of $250,000,000,000. This capital we have not developed; we have overlooked the whole question of its complete and efficient development. . . . We have, then, in developing the physical resources of our country, done the little thing, relatively; it remains now to do the infinitely greater thing, and it remains to the teachers of tomorrow to be of such kind and ability as will be the great creative and administrative force in doing this supremely wonderful thing.[4]

While the Industrial Education movement was an important force in America, its impact on secondary education early in the century never did fully satisfy the interests of its major proponents. Continued opposition by higher education interests, labor groups, public school teachers, and the public at large successfully resisted efforts by many business leaders to turn all or most secondary schools into centers for specialized job training programs. To be sure, vocational education programs were put into place following the Smith-Hughes act of 1917, but they were primarily targeted at urban working-class children or children remaining in agricultural areas. Yet, vocational and agricultural education for the rural and urban "disadvantaged" were argued by their champions as extensions of general education. The most articulate spokespersons for such limited programs frequently talked about the community-building possibilities of such offerings and were quick to argue that vocational and agricultural education would not create overspecialized workers for abuse by the private sector.

On the other hand, there did seem to be a compelling logic behind educational proposals to better link the human resource needs of the workplace with the agenda(s) of public education. Economists were talking about the value of human resources for economic development, and many social scientists maintained that social progress depended upon an ever increasing, specialized and rational division of labor. Furthermore, psychologists and advocates of scientific management models designed many of their programs around notions of individual differences and how such differences could be best exploited for personal and/or industrial success. Advocates of Industrial Education clearly emphasized both of these themes, arguing that there were two distinct types of jobs emerging in the workplace: management/supervisory/technical positions and semiskilled/unskilled jobs (reserved for low status workers) requiring little formal training. On the other hand, even low-status children might need additional schooling, according to some sociologists and psychologists. The now scientifically fashionable concept of "deviance" had entered the vocabulary of "adolescent development." And extended periods of socialization to civilize an earlier generation of what we now categorize as "at risk" students were proposed as an additional thrust of secondary education.

THE "SCIENCES" OF CULTURE-EPOCHS AND OF INDIVIDUAL DIFFERENCES

Increasingly by the turn of the century, social scientists had begun to argue that their understanding of the human factors related to and supportive of social progress had policy implications for American educators. A variety of applied social psychologists, sociologists, and educational psychologists began to provide perspectives on the nature of youth and on how the "needs" and abilities of young people might best be utilized in the workplace. Several of them specifically argued that the mission of the school could quite logically be linked to the needs of the private sector.

Two interrelated interests of early twentieth-century American psychologists, which later would figure prominently in secondary school reform, focused on the nature of child development and individual differences. For example, the scientific validity of the concept of "mental discipline," popular among higher education spokespersons and social Darwinists, was attacked by psychologists like G. Stanley Hall. Hall had discovered, he said, something interesting about the process of child development. No longer did civilization need to base its educational considerations and programs on purely speculative assumptions about what children were like or what they would need. Rather, science and the scientific method could now be used to understand the process of child development. According to Hall and his followers, advances in the science of child development would have direct implications for how school curricula ought to be constructed.

Hall's famous "discovery" regarding the nature of child development was that children's developmental processes seemed to approximate those of cultural evolution. That is, just as the anthropologists and sociologists had been "discovering" the invariable stages of cultural evolution from savagery to modernity, so too children progressed from savagery to adulthood in an ostensibly predictable and invariable sequence. This culture-epochs theory attracted much attention. Hall made one of the first scientifically convincing arguments for curricular differentiation in schooling and argued that the limitations in children's native endowment made using the school to improve society an unnatural act. Importantly, Hall declared that schooling in America had to be scientifically guided by a concern for children's health and happiness. And the best guarantee that children would one day fit into modern society and help it progress was to develop more scientifically informed schooling programs, rather than staying with outdated teaching methods from the past.

> Much of culture-epochs theory's wide appeal in education lay in its association with a scientific order of studies and with the promise it held out for an integration of the curriculum instead of what Hall once referred to as a "mob of subjects.". . . In the case of culture-epochs, the sequence of epochs in human history, and the actual materials for study, were concentrated around the cultural content of those epochs. Thus, while children were in their "savage" stage of development, they would study materials in all their subjects derived from that historical epoch, such as ancient mythology and fables. . . . another of Hall's preoccupations was with what he called "individualization," leading him to prescribe wide variation in what was taught, not only in terms of the great range of intellectual abilities within the school population, but in terms of other genetically determined characteristics such as gender. Nature not only fixed the stages through which all human beings passed, but determined the limits of human educability and, hence, the nature of social heirarchy.[5]

TWO ADDITIONAL PERSPECTIVES
FROM EDUCATIONAL PSYCHOLOGY

The child study movement was intellectually important and related to a number of popular turn-of-the-century pedagogical models. For purposes of our analysis, it was significant because it gave some scientific validity to the argument that children and adults had different competencies, and that such competencies placed limitations on how much individuals could learn even if they applied themselves. Specifically, Hall's work and that of his colleagues helped justify the notion that a diversified curriculum for children of different abilities, of different genders, and of different ages was scientifically defensible. A person's place in life and the process it took to get there were genetically fixed and not subject (only) to hard work or "mental discipline."

However, while different curricular offerings for theoretically different types of children was a theme to be amplified later, Hall's culture-epochs theory was soon challenged by two other emerging psychological perspectives: learning psychology, and the more precise assessment of "human abilities," like intelligence. Learning psychology took serious issue with any supposed theory not based on systematic observation. To be scientific, according to learning psychologists, individual behavior had to be observed and recorded as a prerequisite to analysis. In order to account for different patterns of behavior among individuals, very strict experimental controls needed to be applied. Only in such a way could social scientists prove the impact of particular environments or conditions on individual behavior.

According to one of the movement's founding fathers, Edward Thorndike, learning was defined as the strength of an association between a given stimulus and the organism's response. In addition, various types of rewards for particular behaviors seemed to strengthen the repeatability of any given behavior under carefully controlled conditions. Such observations, students of Thorndike argued, had direct implications for education. One of these was that the learner need not understand material deemed by the teacher as worthy of knowing; as long as the association between a stimulus and response was strengthened by a reinforcer, learning was being facilitated. Relatedly, a second perspective offered by learning psychologists was that the shaping of learner behavior was best accomplished when learner activities were broken down into the smallest possible units.

In essence, the model of teaching and learning proclaimed by learning psychologists was very similiar to the model already emerging in the workplace. There, according to Braverman, work was being divided into the smallest possible units. And there, workers were urged not to reflect upon the meaning of their work or its inherent utility. Instead, successful performance would lead to good ratings and better pay. This link between efficient workshop settings and later classroom settings, while championed under the guise of either management or psychological "science," clearly suggests how the rational concern with worker and student "productivity" was coming to dominate many aspects of human life by the early part of the century.

On another front, the growing science of "human abilities" was very visible in the United States by the 1920s. Attempts at quantifying physiological and cognitive differences between individuals had been a speculative interest among various thinkers since at least the eighteenth century in Europe, but it wasn't until the early twentieth century that verifiable and efficient methods for attempting such assessments were possible. Perhaps the major accomplishment of psychologists interested in cataloging differences in human abilities was their publicly perceived success in constructing the intelligence tests used by the army in World War I. Faced with quickly putting together an army for war in Europe, and having to screen and categorize literally hundreds of thousands of prospective soldiers in a very short time period, psychologists gathered mounds of intelligence data that they correlated with proficiency ratings of soldiers once they were in the field. Based on the success of their correlations, they could now "predict" superior soldiering and inferior soldiering; by the war's end these tests were being used not only to weed out soldiers judged intellectually incompetent to fight and follow orders, but also to help assign enlistees to different positions within the army. In retrospect, even the early intelligence test designers concede the original instruments they used were culturally biased and unfair. Yet it took just a few years for most secondary schools to utilize similarly biased instruments extensively in their educational programs.

IMPLICATIONS OF THE FINDINGS
OF EDUCATIONAL PSYCHOLOGY

The competing scientific perspectives briefly articulated here suggest several interesting points. On the one hand, the popularity of science as a conceptual theme to help guide individual and social development is very significant. No longer, claimed many social and behavioral scientists, should old-fashioned and unscientific notions guide government, business, or educational policy. For example, if advances in scientific measurement could help win "the war to end all wars," surely they could help to engineer an even greater century of progress than had been seen in the nineteenth.

However, a careful reading of the differences between the viewpoints presented here reveals how diverse, fragmented, and methodologically unsophisticated educational psychology was in the first decades of the century. For example, while one group of scientists claimed that adults should allow children to evolve at their own pace, another argued just as strongly that only by carefully monitoring and reinforcing virtually every behavior could there be any guarantee of normal adult performance. Indeed, while one group of scientists argued that individual differences in intelligence were primarily the result of genetic material, another argued with equal force that environmental differences accounted for different adult characteristics. And while one group claimed that the future success of Western culture depended on the scientific testing and allocating of individuals to occupations and careers based on their genetically determined intelligence, another group declared that the environments in which children grew up ought to be carefully structured and routinized so as to create and reinforce the exact kinds of individuals that the culture needed. Each one of these very different competing arguments was made in the name of science.

THE "SCIENCE" OF
EDUCATIONAL ADMINISTRATION

In addition to attempts at developing the study of child development and individual differences, another erstwhile "scientific" pursuit thought relevant to growing demand for educational services was the science of educational administration. The dramatic increase in secondary school enrollments seen from the late nineteenth through the early twentieth centuries was mentioned earlier. In addition, taxpayers were increasingly alarmed by the high number of children who never even completed grade school. Instead of moving quickly through elementary school, many children were held back. In some school systems, for example, it was not atypical for 30 or 40 percent of children at a given grade level to be retained.

Because compulsory education for children had become almost universal by this time and taxpayer costs were continually increasing, concerned citizen groups wanted to know why educators seemed to be having so much trouble socializing children and giving them the basic skills they needed to move on to work or to high school.

By the early twentieth century, institutional crises were at hand in hundreds of school districts of the United States. Demand for schooling was greatly exceeding the resources available for it and no universally agreed-upon school curriculum had been put into place even within schools in the same city, let alone in different parts of the country. According to an emerging breed of educational administrators, however, advances in the science of scientific management first pioneered in the private sector could provide the instructional and organizational answers necessary to solve these institutional crises.

Business leaders and an emerging number of school efficiency experts felt that the problem with schools was that they were inefficient. Efficient business organizations had clearly demarcated chains of command, exact and specific job requirements, and a highly specialized division of labor. Such "scientific" attributes of business (as opposed to the moral values of an earlier era) were argued to be the basis of the principles on which future social progress in the West would continue. And if the school was to either lead or play a part in the continual advance of culture, its organizational practices would have to become more scientific (i.e., efficient). Many school administrators seemed eager to respond to calls for making their operation more "scientifically" sound. In a modern day classic, Raymond Callahan describes the zeal with which school administrators took up the cause of scientific management.

> As early as February, 1911, educators began responding publicly to the demand to apply scientific management to the work of the school. The occasion was the annual meeting of the Department of the Superin-

tendence of the National Education Association, and the administrator who initiated the response was J. George Becht, principal of the State Normal School in Claxton, Pennsylvania. Becht told his audience that the nation had been seeking a more scientific basis for the "common arts of life" for the past twenty-five years. This basis had been found, he said, through the pioneering efforts of Frederick W. Taylor, who had showed what miracles could be achieved "by applying the principles of scientific management to the activities that range from the carrying of a hod to the highest expressions of physical labor".[6]

Scientific management was seen to be useful at the organizational level in several ways. For example, were schools to be run as businesses were, some standardization of outcomes needed to be achieved. Various educators, therefore, sought to specify more clearly what types of learner outcomes needed to be achieved through instruction. For example, some school reformers argued that pupil classroom behaviors ought to be the unit of analysis in education. If student responses (or recitations) were called for as part of the learning process, then pupil–teacher ratios that allowed for the greatest number of teacher-directed recitations at the least cost ought to be the goal. Moreover, if it proved to be the case that some academic specialties (like science) were more expensive to teach than others (like English), school leaders interested in cost effectiveness were frequently urged to alter the way in which the more expensive classes were taught, or perhaps to ration the number of students taking these classes.

Another good example of how concerns for efficiency translated into educational discourse can be seen in the new ways teaching and learning tasks were being discussed during this period. For example, many proponents of scientific management wanted to carefully define and reward teacher work and continually referred to teachers as workers, hoping to equate their work with those now staffing the assembly lines in America. Relatedly, students were seen as "raw material" to be processed by the school, and learning outcomes were typically referred to as products.

As such arguments would suggest, school leaders during the first several decades of the twentieth century were urged by many reformers to concentrate on their organizational and management skills. The school superintendency of the future, such arguments implied, would depend less on the instructional and/or moral leadership attributes that had brought these leaders to the forefront of public education. Rather, the future of the public school and of those who led it would depend on the scientific management skills of school administration, as such management skills had been proven to be the key to current and future economic development and social progress of the nation.

Some prominent school reformers went even further than this. For example, University of Chicago Professor Franklin Bobbitt believed that since the free enterprise system stood for all that was best in America, and since the private sector was far ahead of the schools in applying the lessons of scientific management, school leaders should open their doors and invite business leaders in to help make them more productive and efficient. After all, argued Bobbitt, the products of the educational system needed to be attuned to the needs of business and industry. Again Raymond Callahan summarized a growing consensus among educators regarding the systematic linkage of education and the private sector.

> Having established that standards, and means for measuring them, were necessary and desirable, Bobbitt turned to the question of how they were to be determined. This should be done in education just as in industry. The standards and specifications for steel rails were set by the railroads, not by the steel plants, and the specification for educational products should be set by the community, not by educators. "A school system," he said, "can no more find standards of performance within itself than a steel plant can find the proper height or weight per yard for steel rails from the activities within the plant." Bobbitt went beyond merely suggesting that the business and industrial world enter the schools and set up standards: He made it their civic duty. He stated that through such action the business world would be doing a "valuable service" for the schools . . . .[7]

THE SCIENCE OF EDUCATIONAL ADMINISTRATION AND EQUALITY OF EDUCATIONAL OPPORTUNITY

Making public elementary and secondary schools run more efficiently, however, would prove to be even more difficult than it was for the private sector. The problem was, schools whose teachers had been previously interested in and oriented to a common curriculum for a narrow range of student types were increasingly being asked to educate children coming from many different backgrounds with widely different interests and abilities. Were schools to scientifically (i.e., bureaucratically) structure classroom instruction, upon what types of student interest and abilities would such instructional objectives be based? In fact, how should teachers and administrators themselves be trained to operate in a school setting that more resembled a factory? Education was, after all, more than just job training. Or such had been the message handed down by earlier generations of teachers. And how exactly could the scientific administrator reduce the essence of a Plato or a Shakespeare to a series of cost-effective units?

Monumental as such concerns may seem, they did not deter scientific management disciples in their efforts to scientifically map out the most basic of educational units, to determine how best to hire and train schoolteachers, and to design experimental systems to make schools more closely approximate factories in their day-to-day operations. On the other hand, the concern for equality of educational opportunity so often voiced by prominent educators since the mid-nineteenth century did provide a potential roadblock for many adherents to the scientific management perspective. Thus the most perplexing problem for many school leaders was to figure out a way scientifically and efficiently to design and carry through an educational program that would be both cost-effective and at the same time provide for equality of educational opportunity.

The scientifically based solution to this problem was offered by those psychologists who had earlier helped construct and supposedly validate the I.Q. test used in World War I. Through I.Q. tests specifically directed at school-age populations, it was claimed, all interested parties in a school could benefit. For school administrators, intelligence tests could be used as aids to the smooth operation of school systems by screening and sorting children. In such a way, dullards and average children (supposedly identified by the intelligence tests) could be separated into different classrooms and potential repeaters could be schooled using different techniques.

For individual students, such a process would facilitate more "realistic" learner objectives, thus reducing the frustration that slower learners or faster learners supposedly experienced in classrooms not demanding outcomes appropriate to their inherited intelligence levels. Moreover, equality of educational opportunity could be implemented via the use of I.Q. tests, proponents argued, because such tests would scientifically help to determine the best curricular opportunities for children. Given the great advances in psychological science, it would be unethical and discriminatory not to use intelligence measures to sort and track "disadvantaged" students. By using psychometric data, advocates asserted, school training programs tailored to individual strengths and weaknesses would minimize the potential for failure among poorer children.

Most importantly, the use of I.Q. tests in education could help facilitate economic development of the country, because the specific individual worker characteristics needed for different occupations must obviously be related to differences in human abilities. That is (as Frederick Taylor had emphasized earlier), different types of occupations demanded different levels of intelligence and physical skills. The key to making schools scientifically efficient while at the same time meeting the emerging needs of business and industry was to match assessible student characteristics with the requirements of their future jobs. In this way, the curriculum could be made more relevant and efficient for educators, prevent the "miseducation" of children, and provide ready and willing workers for the private sector.

LEARNING TO BE GOOD CONSUMERS

Finally, there was another link between the private sector and the secondary school in the United States in the early twentieth century. This had to do with the increasing concern among educators that students (typically girls) had to have some consumer skills in order to live in the modern world. As you will recall, one of the important arguments concerning the need for formal schooling was that emerging occupations could not be taught at home. The domestic skills required for running a twentieth-century household could not be learned from previous generations (there were of course no television commercials or talk shows through which Americans could be exposed to new products and how to use them). Therefore, many educators believed that the new time- and labor-saving technologies becoming available to citizens of the United States, as well as new scientifically based knowledge on such things as childrearing, demanded training in "domestic sciences," or as we currently call it, home economics. Thus, by the 1920s the schools had taken on the task of producing specific types of workers for the national economy, as well as the consumers of its products.

SOCIAL SCIENCE CRITICS
OF EDUCATIONAL EFFICIENCY

Neither the theories of scientific management nor those of educational psychology were accepted as the final word in school reform by various civic and educational groups in the early part of the twentieth century. Not all parents were convinced, nor were most leaders in labor or higher education. Since all children theoretically could use emerging tracking patterns in secondary schools to their advantage, visible opponents to many such reforms were fewer than might have been expected. However, there were several important social scientists who felt that serious mistakes were being made in school reform under the guise of science. In the late nineteenth century, for example, the sociologist Lester Frank Ward disagreed strenuously with both the social Darwinists and other cultural evolution theorists. In his opinion, there was a fundamental difference between biological and social evolution. The former, he agreed, was based on random mutation, and led by chance to improved characteristics for individual species. However, he argued, human societies have always bettered themselves through conscious weighing of alternatives and plans of action. He argued that planned (or "telic") evolution was the way of human cultures, and the improved planning now made possible through use of the scientific method held out significant potential for our developing institutions. Furthermore, he perceived deep and serious problems in the America of his day (e.g., crime and poverty) that social institutions ought to be trying to solve, rather than waiting for them to disappear through further economic development.

Another more influential critic of the emerging rationale and programs designed to allow students to better "fit into" America's emerging (and stratified) occupational structure was John Dewey. Interestingly, harking back to older political economy perspectives, Dewey couched his arguments in terms of social and economic science as well as moral philosophy.

Although Dewey was himself a great advocate of science, social progress, and technology, he also recognized the social problems that continual and rapid industrial growth was bringing to America. He believed that reasoned scientific analysis could help solve these problems. For example, Dewey agreed with earlier critics of capitalism, like Robert Owen (almost a century before), that the type of economic development occurring in the West undermined community membership and participation. Dewey also agreed with Emile Durkheim that social life and social cohesion were fundamental building blocks of human existence. However, he disagreed with both of these precursors regarding the implications of these factors for twentieth-century social and educational life.

Specifically, he disagreed with Owen that the loss of community was an insurmountable obstacle to what he perceived as desirable social change. Indeed, he disagreed with Durkheim and his followers about the conservative moral development imperative (character building) for social curricula. Like Ward, Dewey argued that people could reflect upon the implications of progress for the betterment of the human condition. In particular, Dewey believed that the scientific method ought to be taught to children and that they should then use this training to understand and solve social problems themselves, rather than being merely targeted as the object of scientific understanding.

Public school reform for Dewey would include facilitating children's group problem-solving skills. This would both allow them to understand the economic and social evolution of the United States and enable them to help fashion the world to come. The school, argued Dewey, could be used to link emerging technology with its social purpose; could facilitate use of the scientific method in human problem solving; and could demonstrate the importance of collective and democratic processes in such problem solving. In this way, argued Dewey, a new social cohesion could be developed—a cohesion based on future progress under the control of human thought rather than a cohesion based upon previous manipulative traditions. As did several earlier critics of capitalist development, Dewey believed that economic development ought not dictate the social lives of individuals, but ought to serve the interests of society.

CRITICS OF THE UTILITY OF SOCIAL SCIENCE FOR GUIDING EDUCATIONAL POLICY IN THE EARLY TWENTIETH CENTURY

Finally, there were social scientists and philosophers who found in the proposals and language of mainstream social science and its commitment to social progress much irony and even repression. Max Weber, for example, described the transformation in schooling under capitalism as something other than the unfolding of progress or the triumph of democracy. Rather, he was interested in cataloging how older notions of the educated person became transformed under the guise of economic development and the new rationality it called for. Specifically, Weber was concerned with the liberal arts model and how the intellectually well-rounded individual was being replaced with a new and different conception of the "well-educated person." In the "modern" definition, the well-educated person was one highly specialized in very particular professional (occupational) knowledge. He found this to be a historically important transformation. He argued that the social and economic progress supposedly brought forth by capitalism did not liberate humanity from its age-old problems (i.e., inequality and poverty). Rather, it merely substituted new mechanisms of rationalization and control within society and brought forth new sets of power and status relations in the culture.

While Weber argued that there was no remedy for human inequality, Marxist–Leninist scholars remained concerned about what they perceived as the violence done to workers and colonials in the name of American and European social progress and economic development. By the late 1920s a variety of writers in the Marxist tradition (like Antonio Gramsci in Italy and Max Horkheimer in Germany) had become quite interested in how the ideology of social progress and capitalist economic development was coming to dominate the language and beliefs of citizens in capitalist nations. To such writers, the adoption of "bourgeois" social science to help make public schooling better meet the needs of capitalist leaders was not merely a convenience. As Marx had predicted, it was just one more step in the linking up of all social agencies with the needs of capitalist economic development.

SUMMARY AND DISCUSSION

Much of the current rhetoric regarding the potential contribution of education for economic development in this country suggests that somehow our schools have rarely been involved in this pursuit. As this and the preceding chapters have outlined, such is not the case. Economists up to and including those of the nineteenth century were interested in the value of human resources for economic development. Yet, their academic, scientific, and political interests did not focus on the school's potential in teaching worker skills. These were seen as acquired primarily in the private sector. And operations of the private sector were to be only minimally interfered with (or aided) by government, according to neoclassical economists.

Most social scientists, on the other hand, believed that economic development was important and could be enhanced by attention to the social implications of economic growth. They typically argued that social problems occurred with capitalist development; yet such problems could be alleviated through the application of scientific methods and understanding. Public schools, facing much growth and demand throughout the late nineteenth and early twentieth century, (selectively) borrowed ideas and proposals of sociologists, social psychologists, and psychologists. Most of these perspectives were consistent with capitalist notions of the increasing necessity for specialized skill training and with teaching children that their vocational futures lay in securing a satisfactory job within a large company. In other words, most educational and business leaders at the turn of the century assumed that economic development and social progress went hand in hand, and they continued in the earlier tradition of attempting to educate students in accord with their understanding of the role of education in economic development.

A few more critical social scientists were convinced that using the public school to "help" students fit into jobs and become consumers as desired by leaders of the private sector was a grave mistake. Continuing other criticisms of the supposed benefits of economic development, such social scientists and educators held out hopes that public education could be an arena for serious reflection on the social costs as well as opportunities of economic growth. Social science, and the school, according to some believers, could be used to change the way the private sector worked and need not serve only as a source for legitimizing the status quo.

Finally, a few radical social theorists continued to note how new status distinctions and ideologies were coming to dominate social relations as capitalism matured. Max Weber wrote about how emerging curricular specialization in American and European schools was redefining the very concept of education to one of technical rationality. Meanwhile, students of Marx began to point out that the economic rationality necessary for capitalism to survive and prosper was increasingly being utilized to construct institutions like the school, and to influence the way people in Western cultures were coming to define the meaning of social life.

Up until the early twentieth century, school reforms attempting to link the purpose of public schooling with the requirements of economic development had been primarily championed by local business and civic leaders and by educators. It wasn't until 1917 that the federal government formally became involved in vocational education with the passage of the Smith–Hughes Act. However, in the next several decades, even greater attention to the possibilities of using the school for purposes of economic development would be advocated by economists and social scientists. And state and federal agencies would come to play an increasingly large role in this tenuous relationship.

NOTES

1. C. H. Edson, "Schooling for Work and Working for School: Perspectives on Immigration and Working Class Education in Urban America, 1880–1920," in R. Everhart (ed.), *The Public School Monopoly*. Cambridge, MA: Ballinger Publishing, 1982, p. 153.
2. Lawrence Cremin, *The Transformation of The School*. New York: Random House, 1964, pp. 95–96.
3. Marvin Lazerson and W. Norton Grubb, *American Education and Vocationalism: A Documentary History*. New York: Teachers College Press, 1974, pp. 90–92.
4. *Ibid.*, p. 92.
5. Herbert Kliebard, *The Struggle for the American Curriculum: 1893–1958*. Boston: Routledge & Kegan Paul, 1986. pp. 45–47.
6. Raymond Callahan, *Education and the Cult of Efficiency*. Chicago. University of Chicago Press, 1962, p. 54.
7. *Ibid.*, p. 83.

FOR ADDITIONAL READING

In addition to the historical accounts listed in the Notes and in Chapter 3, several other reviews of important ideas mentioned in the preceding chapter are worth studying. A good attempt to review the competing notions many social scientists held regarding the nature of social progress and how the school might be structured to effect it can be found in Blaine Mercer and Herbert Covey, *Theoretical Frameworks in the Sociology of Education* (Cambridge, MA: Schenkman Publishing, 1982). Attempts to assess human intelligence with regard to its (typically misguided) policy implications is available in Stephen Jay Gould's *Mismeasure of Man* (New York: W. W. Norton, 1981). Collections of the educational thinking of various social scientists and other academics like John Dewey, William T. Harris, G. Stanley Hall, and Herbert Spencer are available in the *Classics in Education* series, published by Teachers College Press (New York: various dates). A good collection of the various social scientific works related to education by Max Weber is available in H. Gerth and C. Wright Mills (eds.) *From Max Weber: Essays in Sociology* (New York: Oxford University Press, 1946). Emile Durkheim's works on the division of labor in society and on education are both highlighted in *Emile Durkheim: Selected Writings,* edited by Anthony Giddens (Cambridge: Cambridge University Press, 1972). Early work in the Marxist-inspired area of critical theory is reviewed in David Held's *Introduction to Critical Theory* (Berkeley, CA: University of California Press, 1980), and the work of Antonio Gramsci can be found in Harold Entwistle's *Antonio Gramsci* (London: Routledge & Kegan Paul, 1979).

CHAPTER 6

Children as Resources: Human Capital Theory, Modernization Theories, and the School

We have already traced early interests in the fields of economics and social science, particularly as they related to formal education. Both of these traditions have clearly influenced educational theory and practice as espoused by professional educators and business and civic leaders within many local school districts during the past hundred and fifty years. However, only during the past several decades have perspectives of economists and social scientists been used explicitly by state and national agencies and groups in the United States to inform educational policy. This chapter is concerned with how human capital theory, modernization theory, and the vision of a post-industrial society are coming to influence contemporary notions of American school reform.

Our interest here is to explain the social and economic conditions that gave rise to the idea that the state and federal governments in the United States should be specifically involved in public education. Then, we will attempt to provide some insight into human capital theory and modernization theory, as these two perspectives have recently come to inform many educational policy proposals. In so doing, we will be able to show how earlier theories and models relating education to economic and social development have "come of age" during our time. Such an analysis will clarify the discussion of specific reform proposals visible in education today (see Chapter 7).

THE GREAT DEPRESSION AND
THE EMERGENCE OF THE STATE
IN ECONOMIC DEVELOPMENT POLICY

As we closed Chapter 5, the American economy seemed to be growing and developing rapidly. To be sure, several severe economic depressions occurred during this time period, and there were frequent worker strikes, high levels of unemployment among immigrants and minorities, and social problems brought about by rapid demographic shifts in the United States. Typically, such problems were pronounced as transitional ones and/or ones that social scientists espousing programs like social efficiency could solve. However, the Wall Street collapse of 1929 and the subsequent depression greatly altered many of the optimistic notions Americans had about the unlimited prospects for economic development.

According to neoclassical economics at the turn of the twentieth century, the Great Depression should never have occurred. That is, while economic lulls and recessions were possible (and inevitable), market forces would always cause the economy to rebound after a brief period. Recessions, it was argued, came about when consumer demand was low. Instead of purchasing goods and services, people put their money into savings. However, when people were not consuming the products of domestic industries, fewer sales forced business owners to reduce inventories, lay off workers, and become more timid in borrowing for investment in their productive capacities.

In times of recession, interest rates would continually drop until more aggressive firms began to reinvest in new plant capacities and product lines, when the rates on savings would fall so low as to make borrowing very attractive. After all, banks could not lend money to the private sector unless the terms for borrowing became appealing. And sooner or later, reasoned neoclassical economists, people would also have to re-enter the marketplace for new or replacement consumer goods.

But the Great American Depression of the 1930s did not quickly subside as most economists early on predicted. Indeed, many individuals lost all of the savings they might have been able to live on during the recession due to the epidemic of bank failures in the early 1930s. Thus many would-be consumers were financially unable to help bring the United States out of the depression: they simply had no money saved to purchase the goods in order to stimulate the national economy. Worse yet, many Americans had no "safety nets" to help them through this period: no work, no savings, no workman's compensation, no welfare programs, nor any other well-developed social service schemes that could come to the systematic rescue of increasing numbers of the unemployed, homeless, and poor.

Policy makers seeking the help of economists to explain and/or alleviate causes and effects of the Depression found most of them just as perplexed about the situation as anyone else. After all, the beneficence of capitalist development in the United States had for almost a century been accepted as God's gift to humanity; it was believed that our economic system could only get better as the best minds in economics and social science guided it. At the one extreme were the most conservative of economists, whose advice was to do nothing, because sooner or later the system would self-correct and return to equilibrium. At the other extreme were various socialist groups who had for decades been predicting the collapse of capitalism. And in between were economists frequently too specialized within particular research traditions to venture much advice on any systemwide solution to the ills that plagued America in the 1930s.

The one important and prestigious economist who did venture a novel interpretation of the problem, as well as make specific proposals to get Western economies moving again, was John Maynard Keynes. According to Keynes, capitalist economies did in fact move toward equilibrium, as almost every neoclassical economist agreed. However, reasoned Keynes, such an equilibrium need not move always toward full production and employment. Economic periods could in fact be relatively stable with minimal or no growth as well as high unemployment.

Believing that this was the cause of the continuing depression in Britain and the United States, he reasoned that the governments of both nations had to help stimulate their domestic economies in order to overcome the worldwide depression. What Keynes called for was direct government intervention in the economic process. Specifically, Keynes argued (in America) that the federal government ought to borrow money from the banks, set up a variety of public works projects to undertake nationally important tasks, and hire many of the increasing numbers of unemployed to work on those projects.

In so doing, not only would vital civic works be undertaken (like conservation projects in the national parks, and sponsorship of folk artists and folklorists attempting to capture and record how Americans in different regions of the nation lived in the twentieth century, etc.), but more importantly, money put back into the hands of workers would cause consumer demand to rise again. And with increasing consumer demand, as most other economists recognized, America's factories would again begin to produce more goods, and enterprising capitalists would again have faith that whatever worthwhile products they could put into production would find a market.

Of course, many industrialists and manufacturers were either unsure of such radical proposals, or downright opposed to them. And many economists disagreed with Keynes. Direct government intervention in the system, they argued, wouldn't work, and would possibly throw out of balance a self-regulating system that had a hundred years' proven track record, or would lead only to further intervention in the market. By all accounts, according to many critics, such proposals were socialistic and not to be tried in the United States.

EMERGING DISPUTES AMONG MID-TWENTIETH-CENTURY ECONOMISTS

As was mentioned earlier, theoretical disputes among economists and political economists had existed quietly throughout the nineteenth and into the twentieth centuries. Neoclassical economics, which attempted to explain economic development with regard to individual market decisions, was clearly dominant during this period. The economic crises of Western nations during the 1920s and 1930s, however, were responsible for bringing into prominence some alternative and sometimes competing perspectives by the time of the Second World War. Ross Harrold, for example, maintains that at least five distinct economic schools of thought exist currently within the discipline.[1] These include the still dominant neoclassical school, Keynesian economics, the institutional school, the political economy school, and Marxist economics. Another attempt to categorize current schools of thought is undertaken by Cole, Cameron, and Edwards.[2] They differentiate among those subscribing to the "subjective preference theory of value," those preferring the "cost of production theory of value," and those believing in the "abstract labor theory of value." Of course other scholars attempting to describe the historical and contemporary scene in economics have proposed their own outlines of the contending camps.[3]

It would of course be impossible in a work of this type to systematically compare and contrast all of the issues and interpretations that give rise to debates among economists, although much of this book relates to such debates. For our purposes here, what is important about such arguments is the emergence in the 1930s of new economic models following the failure of many neoclassical economists to adequately predict or provide insight into how to restore the American economy. Specifically, the compelling theories offered by Keynes as well as the qualified success and popular approval of government sponsored work projects gave new life to those political leaders interested in using the power of state and national governments to intervene and help stimulate economic growth through a variety of measures.

As we have discussed, one of the major beliefs among neoclassical economists is that the state ought not to get involved in the economic process, except to settle disputes between manufacturers and to ensure that workers' rights were protected. But the proposals of the Keynesians were exactly the opposite, and many of the more conservative economists bitterly complained about the growing presence of the state and its interference with the economic process. According to many other less ideologically rigid economists, however, governments in advanced industrialized nations had for years been aiding in various ways the economic development of their nations. For example, protective tariffs had been put into place by many governments of these developing nations when they were needed to protect fledgling industries.

Additionally, various national security interests and economic development needs had been sponsored and paid for out of public resources when they were judged too costly for private businesses to underwrite. For example, national defense, ostensibly of benefit to all citizens as well as to the interests of business, is frequently judged a public rather than a private expense. Likewise, transportation systems like rivers, railroads, and highways have been seen to be an underlying prerequisite to the distribution of every manufacturer's products and the fulfilling of every consumer's demands. Thus, our government, as well as most others, was and is heavily involved in subsidizing these aspects of the nation's economic infrastructure.

According to other twentieth-century economists, most of the domestic economies in advanced capitalist nations were increasingly coming under the control of small groups of companies rather than the small business entrepreneurs envisioned by nineteenth-century economists. Most of the large chemical, steel, and automobile production in the United States, for example, was controlled by fewer than half a dozen companies as early as the 1930s, a fact not well publicized by neoclassical economists. Furthermore, noted some observers, the growing control of a few companies over selected markets meant that frequently they could control the prices set for their goods, making them less competitive in the long run than products of businesses in other market sectors.

By the middle of the twentieth century, then, it had become quite apparent that the modern state had become heavily involved in the dynamics of most national economies. Furthermore, with the growing popularity of Keynesian economics, increasing numbers of policy leaders began to look to the field of economics for advice on how the government could play even greater, more positive roles in stimulating economic growth in both advanced and developing countries.

THE GOVERNMENT
AND MONETARY POLICY

In point of fact, the combination of exasperation with a long standing depression and the advice of economists like Keynes led to a variety of New Deal programs under the Roosevelt administration to get money back into the hands of consumers via public works projects. In addition, a Social

Security system was also put into effect, whereby even more money could be put into the hands of those unable to work. By this system, money borrowed by the government from the banks, which would be combined later with taxes on the current generation of workers, was put back into the economy in the form of spendable income for the elderly and disabled; this in turn was to influence consumer demand.

While the actual economic benefits of the proposals made by Keynes and the policies adopted by the United States during the 1930s are still debated by economists near the end of the twentieth century, the idea that the federal government could or should have a role in helping to manage national economic affairs has increasingly become a reality in national policy. We still have a variety of social programs, for example, to put spendable income into the hands of various categories of consumers. Besides, a popular tool of economic management in use during the past several decades has been the increasing of government control over the supply of money circulating in the national economy.

Again, many economists agree that interest rates are a prime factor in decisions of industrialists to build new plants and manufacture new goods. If interest rates are too high, and capitalists have to pay too much interest for the money they would use to expand, then they may forestall such plans. Should this be the case nationwide, it is believed, a recession is bound to follow. If, on the other hand, interest rates are too low, consumers would have less incentive to save, and their increasing demand on consumer goods theoretically would lead to high levels of inflation. In order to stabilize and moderate boom and bust cycles in the economy, therefore, the government has during the past several decades attempted to control the amount of money in circulation. According to the economist John Kenneth Galbraith, the process is not complicated:

> Although economists have derived much useful prestige from the mystery which is supposed to surround monetary policy, in essentials it is rather simple. Savings deposited with the banks or other financial institutions are, of course, available for relending. The amount that is so available can be extended by allowing the banks to borrow from the central bank—in the United States, the Federal Reserve System. This can be encouraged, as necessary, by a favorable lending (rediscount) rate. By buying government securities from the banks, thus leaving them with the money, the supply of funds which they have for lending can be further enhanced by the central bank. If the need is for contraction of demand, the process can be reversed.[4]

The net effect of Keynesian economics and the increasing involvement of the U.S. government in the day-to-day affairs of the economy is thus to bring about a new era in the relationship between the private and public sectors. Specifically, economists like Galbraith would argue, no longer do capitalist economies operate as neoclassical advocates would like us to believe. Increasingly, the state has taken a major role in influencing economic growth since the Great Depression, under the guise that some form of economic planning or forecasting is necessary to ensure future growth. And while such perspectives originated during the Depression years, they became even further elaborated in economic theory and government policy following World War II.

THE ECONOMIC CONSEQUENCES
OF WORLD WAR II

By most accounts, government borrowing and spending in order to help defeat Germany, Japan, and Italy in the Second World War brought the United States completely out of the Depression and illustrated again the crucial role central governments could play in helping to stabilize and stimulate controlled economic growth. World War II created a huge demand for war-related products, the costs of which were borne by taxpayers and the federal government. With a dramatic increase in the production of war-related materiel, full employment (with relatively low wages) was the result. At the same time, the rationing of consumer goods meant that soldiers, as well as civilians now participating in war-related industries, had little to consume, except war bonds issued by the government. Of course, this meant that the government had even more money to put back into spending for the war effort.

At the end of the war, however, new problems loomed over domestic economic development. Specifically, now that soldiers and sailors were to be sent home, what would the nation do with all of these newly "unemployed"? Moreover, how would all the production facilities previously geared to turning out the products of war make the transition back to the production of peacetime products? Importantly, the federal government helped bridge the economic return to peacetime in several ways. For example, low cost mortgage loans for ex-G.I.s were underwritten by the government, which allowed returning soldiers to buy new homes with a very small down payment and at subsidized interest rates. Coupled with new federal and state highway construction programs linking new housing subdivisions with industrial centers, this federal strategy created a huge demand in the housing industry, which subsequently led to a boom in related employment industries (e.g., automobiles and household appliances).

Another program designed to ease potential workers back into a peacetime economy was the G.I. bill. This program guaranteed returning members of the armed forces extensive educational benefits for higher education. The logic underlying such an effort was that currently growing consumer industries would take several years to absorb unemployed soldiers and sailors. Instead of paying lots of unemployment benefits to such people, it was hoped that they would return to school and improve their job skills, until such time as they could be absorbed back into the emerging economy.

On yet another front, it was argued that the maintenance of a beefed-up military presence around the world was necessary for a more permanent peace. Moreover, federal expenditures for continual development of modern weapons and a space program were held out as a good way to ensure that the United States would not be attacked again. In current times, such an argument is frequently couched in the slogan "peace through strength." But however it is conceptualized militarily, the net effect on the economy is that the federal government helps maintain many defense-related industries through defense-related contracts.

THE REBUILDING OF EUROPE AND THE ORIGINS OF CONTEMPORARY HUMAN CAPITAL THEORY

While economists had from time to time reflected upon the quality of the workforce in discussions of economic development, it was really only during the reconstruction of European economies that the human factor in redevelopment became of serious interest to economists. Several economists, like Keynes, had argued following World War I that the severe economic sanctions placed on Germany and its allies after that war would lead to future problems. And in retrospect, his analysis became a shared one among many economic and political leaders as World War II broke out less than twenty years later. Therefore, following World War II, Western leaders came to believe that helping Europe rebuild its industries and restore stable economies there would prevent future cataclysmic events. The Marshall Plan, through which the victors of World War II would finance the rebuilding of the economies of the defeated, was instituted during the postwar years. Under this plan, the United States loaned a great deal of money to Germany and Japan to help restore their national economies.

Astonishingly, in fewer than twenty years, (West) Germany made tremendous strides in restoring its domestic economy—especially given the virtually complete destruction of its infrastructure and manufacturing capabilities by the American assault in the mid 1940s. Many economists were at a loss to explain how Germany's gross national product—or the combined value of all its goods and services—could possibly have become so great in such a short time period. By the 1960s, not only was Germany able to produce most of its domestic needs, but it was also becoming dominant in its exports—thus once again competing with the United States in international markets. On another front, the Japanese economy had similarly rebounded significantly during this period, and soon became a strong economic competitor against the very countries that had helped to make its economic recovery possible.

According to Theodore Schultz, economists asked to gauge the possibility of substantial economic recovery for Europe immediately after the war were less than optimistic. However, Schultz argued, this was the result of their serious underestimation of the importance of the human factor in determining economic development.

> The toll from bombing was all too visible in the factories laid flat, the railroad yards, bridges, and harbors wrecked, and cities in ruin. Structures, equipment and inventories were all heaps of rubble. Not so visible, yet large, was the toll from wartime depletion of the physical plant that escaped destruction by bombs. Economists were called upon to assess the implications of these wartime losses for recovery. In retrospect, it is clear that [we] overestimated the prospective retarding effects of these losses. . . . We fell into this error, I am convinced, because we did not have a concept of *all* capital and, therefore, failed to take account of human capital and the important part that it plays in production in a modern economy.[5]

By the mid-1950s, economists began to redouble their efforts to measure and understand the significance of human skills in the economic development process. As mentioned earlier, such efforts had been made intermittently among the ranks of neoclassical economists throughout the nineteenth and early twentieth century. In efforts to retrace even earlier versions of human capital thinking, economists Elchanan Cohn, B. F. Kiker, and Mary Jean Bowman all attempted to find the roots of contemporary human capital theory.[6] Although discussions of population quality and human skills were present in the works of eighteenth- and nineteenth-century political economists, Cohn points out that such topics were of concern even in early Christian writings. Yet, according to these economists, the practical utility of investing in human resources based on economic theory was rarely appreciated until after World War II.

Mary Jean Bowman suggests that "human capital revolution in economic thought" actually began in the 1890s, because it was then that human creativity in the workplace first became a concern in economic theory. The key factor responsible for making this concept "revolutionary" was the idea that both the private and (later) the public sector might benefit from investments in the development of workers' skills. Irving Fisher, from whom we heard earlier in behalf of the industrial education movement, was perhaps the first economist to link schooling (as opposed to occupational training or apprenticeship) with economic development. According to Bowman, it is in Fisher's analysis of the components of capital that human capital formation receives its first serious twentieth-century attention:

Capital is something (a stock) that yields a flow of services over time. Whether the physical entity in which the capital stock is embodied can be bought and sold is a matter of degree (in modern terminology, degree of "liquidity"), and is not a defining criterion. But resources put into schooling are (among other things) investments in the acquisition of potential future income streams, whether looked at from the individual or from the societal points of view. This is a kind of capital formation. It is the formation of human capital in that the stock that will yield the future income streams is embodied in human beings.[7]

Historically speaking, then, political economists from the late eighteenth and early nineteenth century saw little utility for economic productivity in public schooling. Neoclassical economists first ignored and then began to flirt with academic and abstract notions of people as possessors of skills that might be considered a form of capital. But following World War II, economists began to argue for the practical utility of viewing people as resources, as is evidenced in the number of research papers on the economics of education appearing in the professional journals after 1954. Of the approximately 420 works on this topic discovered by the economist Mark Blaug (written during the twentieth century to 1964), over 90 percent were authored between 1954 and 1964.[8]

CURRENT HUMAN CAPITAL CONCERNS AND THEIR RELATED POPULATION QUALITY FEATURES

It should be noted that education was but one of several "population quality" features of human societies that economists began to quantify during the 1950s, 1960s, and 1970s. Of particular concern to those believing that the quality of human resources determines economic productivity have been those emphasizing the importance of adequate health and nutritional standards and resources for target populations. Theodore Schultz, for example, continues to be an advocate of investment in programs for enhancing national nutritional standards, infant health care services, maternal health programs, etc., not necessarily because people ought to benefit from the success of any national economy, but because healthy, well fed, and well educated people are more likely to contribute to economic development than are sick, malnourished, or uneducated citizens. In point of fact, such arguments were instrumental in the creation of a variety of compensatory programs mounted in the schools and communities as part of President Johnson's "War on Poverty" programs of the 1960s.[9] (See Table 6.1.)

Expanding educational opportunities to more and more citizens in

TABLE 6.1. TOTAL EXPENDITURES OF EDUCATIONAL INSTITUTIONS, BY LEVEL AND CONTROL OF INSTITUTION: UNITED STATES, 1899–1900 TO 1986–87 (IN MILLIONS)

School year	Total	Elementary and Secondary Schools			Colleges and Universities		
		Total	Public	Private[1]	Total	Public	Private
1	2	3	4	5	6	7	8
1899–1900	—	—	$215	—	—	—	—
1909–10	—	—	426	—	—	—	—
1919–20	—	—	1,036	—	—	—	—
1929–30	—	—	2,317	—	$632	$292	$341
1939–40	—	—	2,344	—	758	392	367
1949–50	$8,911	$6,249	5,838	$411	2,662	1,430	1,233
1951–52	10,735	7,861	7,344	517	2,874	1,565	1,309
1953–54	13,147	9,733	9,092	641	3,414	1,912	1,502
1955–56	15,907	11,727	10,955	772	4,180	2,348	1,832
1957–58	20,055	14,525	13,569	956	5,530	3,237	2,293
1959–60	23,860	16,713	15,613	1,100	7,147	3,904	3,244
1961–62	28,503	19,673	18,373	1,300	8,830	4,919	3,911
1963–64	34,440	22,825	21,325	1,500	11,615	6,558	5,057
1965–66	43,682	28,048	26,248	1,800	15,634	9,047	6,588
1967–68	55,652	35,077	32,977	2,100	20,575	12,750	7,824
1969–70	68,459	43,183	40,683	2,500	25,276	16,234	9,041
1970–71	75,741	48,200	45,500	2,700	27,541	18,028	9,513

Year							
1971–72	80,672	50,950	48,050	2,900	29,722	19,538	10,184
1972–73	86,875	54,952	51,852	3,100	31,923	21,144	10,779
1973–74	95,396	60,370	56,970	3,400	35,026	23,542	11,484
1974–75	108,664	68,846	64,846	4,000	39,818	26,966	12,852
1975–76	118,706	75,101	70,601	4,500	43,605	29,736	13,869
1976–77	126,417	79,194	74,194	5,000	47,223	31,997	15,226
1977–78	137,042	86,544	80,844	5,700	50,498	34,031	16,467
1978–79	148,308	93,012	86,712	6,300	55,296	37,110	18,187
1979–80	165,627	103,162	95,962	7,200	62,465	41,434	21,031
1980–81	182,849	112,325	104,125	8,200	70,524	46,559	23,965
1981–82	197,801	120,486	111,186	9,300	77,315	50,813	26,502
1982–83	212,081	128,725	118,425	10,300	83,356	54,338	29,018
1983–84	228,597	139,000	127,500	11,500	89,597	58,124	31,473
1984–85[2]	247,157	148,900	136,500	12,400	98,257	63,704	34,553
1985–86[1]	266,200	160,800	147,600	13,200	105,400	68,200	37,100
1986–87[1]	282,100	170,000	156,000	14,000	112,100	72,600	39,500

[1] Estimated.
[2] Preliminary

NOTES: Blank indicates data not available. Total expenditures for public elementary and secondary schools include current expenditures, interest on school debt and capital outlay. Data for private elementary and secondary schools are estimated. Total expenditures for colleges and universities include current-fund expenditures and additions for plant value. Excludes expenditures of noncollegiate postsecondary institutions. Because of rounding, details may not add to totals. (*Source: Center for Education Statistics, Digest of Education Statistics, Office of Educational Research and Improvement, U.S. Dept. of Education [Washington, DC: U.S. Government Printing Office, May 1987] p. 25.*)

various age groups is also typically called for by human capital theorists. Current human capital theorists usually argue that lack of information regarding educational opportunities and costs sometimes hinders individual investment decisions. That is, since such economists assume individual rationality, they usually declare that people's failure to undertake educational training that would increase the value of their skills probably stems from a lack of knowledge about educational opportunities and how their skills might be marketed afterward. In order to increase potential skill levels among workers, then, greater educational opportunities are always desirable (unless other capital investments are judged to have priority in economic development equations).

Another less well advertised feature of human capital arguments, at least as heard today, concerns the geographical distribution of productive talent within an economy. Human capital theorists typically assume that economic development decisions are both national and individual ones rather than regional ones. By upgrading one's skill, the argument runs, one is then able to pursue more advantageous employment somewhere within the structure of economic opportunities, wherever they are. Making productive use of individual talent within a large and geographically spread-out economy (such as ours) therefore calls for readily available information about where (i.e., in what city) one's newly developed skills are most marketable.

MODERN SOCIOLOGICAL
THEORIES OF DEVELOPMENT

Social scientists as well as economists continued to be interested in economic development during the middle of the twentieth century. As before, however, while most economists continued to assume individual rationality in the economic decision-making process, social scientists remained concerned with the organizational and attitudinal impacts of developing economies upon individuals, and vice versa. Within these traditions two interrelated "functionalist" perspectives began to emerge in social science. Both of these traditions focused on the nature of social change—one emphasized the sociopolitical and individual factors necessary for "modernization" among less developed countries; the other, the emerging personal, social, and economic needs of a "post-industrial society." Both of these themes were related to earlier convictions among social scientists that the social processes of economic development were more complicated than the economists believed.

Social scientists interested in the dynamics of modernization, for example, argued that traditional social structures, economies, and cultures in many non-Western nations operate in significantly different ways from those in Western nations. Some argued, echoing Max Weber, that *individual* freedom, *individual* salvation, mastery over nature, and *individual* consumer satisfaction are in fact cornerstones of Western culture, and certainly predate capitalism in the West. However, in many non-Western cultures the norms and values that underlie personal and economic relations have been found to be quite different. A number of anthropologists, for example, have shown that many non-Western cultures which identify more closely with nature may contain much more intense tribal and family kinship systems and may specify individual role behavior based on ascriptive factors like gender and ethnic status, and so on than do Western cultures. Thus the underlying individual and rational assumptions upon which economists have con-structed their market-oriented theories in the West frequently do not describe the social and interpersonal relationships among people from other cultures.

This view did not necessarily imply for many social scientists that developing nations could not become "modern," nor that "modernization" was not desirable. Rather, it presented a problem for social scientists to understand and a process by which to advise nations interested in de-veloping their economies along Western models. While their ideas did not strictly conform to older cultural evolution theories, those interested in the process of modernization basically continued to equate twentieth-century Western capitalism with both social and economic progress, especially since government involvement in the economy would stave off most of the exploitive conditions of earlier economic periods. According to C. E. Black:

> [modernization] refers to the dynamic form that the age-old process of innovation has assumed as a result of the explosive proliferation of knowledge in recent centuries. It owes its special significance both to its dynamic character and to the universality of its impact on human affairs. It stems initially from an attitude, a belief that society can and should be transformed, that change is desirable. If a definition is necessary, "mod-ernization" may be defined as the process by which historically evolved institutions are adapted to the rapidly changing functions that reflect the unprecedented increase in man's knowledge, permitting control over his environment, that accompanied the scientific revolution. This process of adaption had its origins and initial influence in the societies of Western Europe, but in the nineteenth and twentieth centuries these changes have been extended to all other societies and have resulted in a wordwide transformation affecting all human relationships.[10]

Assuming that Western societies and Western economies were to be desired, social scientists interested in helping to "modernize" developing countries quickly focused on the socialization powers of the school to instill values and skills deemed necessary for social and economic progress. The sociologists Alex Inkeles and David Smith, for example, argued that in order for a nation to develop a sound economy and a modern society, modern character traits needed to be developed among its citizens. Such character traits (e.g., openness to new experiences, future orientation, occupational aspirations, planning for the future, comprehension of economic production, etc.), they felt, were and could be acquired in a number of modern institutional contexts. In a major six-nation study of institutional and media impact on individual modernity, Inkeles and Smith found the school to have the most significant and dramatic impact on their modernity measures in all six countries:

> Our data show unambiguously that the schools in each of our six developing countries [clearly] had a substantial effect on the pupils exposed to their influence. Their pupils did learn. Furthermore, they learned more than reading, writing, and figuring. Our tests show that they also learned values, attitudes and ways of behaving highly relevant to their personal development and to the future of their countries. . . . They had a different sense of time, and a stronger sense of personal and social efficacy; participated more actively in communal affairs; were more open to new ideas, new experiences and new people; interacted differently with others, and showed more concern for subordinates and minorities. They valued science more, accepted change more readily, and were more prepared to limit the number of children they would have. In short, by virtue of having had more formal schooling, their personal character was decidedly more modern.[11]

Character traits associated with entrepreneurship and economic development were also the focus for a number of social psychologists during the 1950s and 1960s. David McClelland, for example, argued that economic success and social progress in the West during the twentieth century could not be taken for granted, as most neoclassical economists had assumed. Rather, argued McClelland, the entrepreneurship qualities upon which modern Western economies had been built were the result of the personality structure of individuals within our cultures. Achievement motivation, or the need for achievement by significant numbers of the population, was the foundation on which economic development had been built in the past, and would be built in the future.

> In a number of empirical studies of achievement motivation, McClelland [called] attention to the correspondence between characteristics attributed to entrepreneurs and characteristics evinced by persons highly motivated to achieve. Their motive is not money for its own sake, but rather for generalized success where money is simply the objective measure of degree of success. They appear to be independent-minded and autonomous. They seek out situations which allow them to have a feeling of personal responsibility for the outcome and where the results of their efforts are clearly measurable.[12]

Significantly, McClelland argued that achievement motivation was learned in the home and in the school: in other words, that the need for achievement was and could be "programmed" into individuals. And McClelland set up a number of adult training programs for leaders of developing countries in the hope that economic development around the world might be enhanced by altering the personality characteristics of businessmen operating in less developed countries.

Achievement norms were also central to highly developed and modern societies according to Talcott Parsons, perhaps America's most influential sociologist of the mid-twentieth century. Parsons argued that modern societies contained highly differentiated formal organizations, and that within such organizations the rules that governed interpersonal interaction were complex, highly impersonal, and contingent on the specialized training of those occupying different roles within them. Also according to Parsons, the reason why some nations were economically and socially advanced while others were not was a function of the effect of cultural differences on norms (like achievement) that they exhibited.

Robert Dreeben, a student of Parsons, also paid particular attention to the topic of norms in his analysis of the contribution public schooling did and should make in preparing individuals for modern life. Dreeben declared that four commonly accepted and acted upon norms of people in highly industrial cultures were necessary. These included achievement orientation, independence, universalism, and specificity. Life in modern, highly industrial, occupationally diverse, and urban societies depended on each individual's setting high standards for work that was frequently to be undertaken alone and very narrowly focused.

Furthermore, argued Dreeben, people in modern cultures need to behave toward others as members of transitional "categories," depending on the situation at hand. The only places in most modern societies where individuals could be socialized into behaving "appropriately" were schools. Dreeben therefore pointed out that public schools did much more than teach academic and technical skills. In fact, he argued, they were inefficient places to teach academic matters—but schools were essential places for helping students to internalize social norms.[13]

Another theme of Parsons and some of his students lay in the area of social stratification, or the relationship between formal training, occupational success, and human ability. Such a theme was addressed earlier in the century (see Chapters 4 and 5) under the guise of individual differences in intelligence. However, the structural–functional school of sociology was interested in the matter of why some occupations paid higher salaries and had greater prestige than others; they would not accept the quasi-scientific explanations that had been popular earlier in the century. Social stratification was judged socially necessary, according to this emergent view, because societies had particular functions and requirements crucial to their stability and growth. Therefore, monetary and prestige inducements were necessary in society to attract those with the most talent into the most socially important positions. Those with less talent or who had less interest in achievement, on the other hand, would find their places in life doing perhaps less interesting but still socially important duties. After all, the logic went, society needs both physicians *and* garbage collectors. Differences in economic and prestige returns to such positions, however, was and ought to be a function of the differences in talent necessary to perform on these different levels.

MERITOCRATIC THEORY AND
THE POST-INDUSTRIAL SOCIETY

Sociological theories about the individual and social precursors to social and economic change were not limited in the 1950s, 1960s, and 1970s to discussions about less developed countries. Extending such arguments partially inherited from earlier in the century, many social scientists such as Theodore Schultz, convinced that our economic, social, and political systems were progressive and understandable, began to suggest how their insights could be used to accelerate social progress.

In the United States and Great Britain, two functionalist sociological perspectives began to reinforce human capital arguments regarding the importance of information to a modern and post-modern economy. According to "meritocratic" theory, success of an advanced economy and social progress depended on bringing the fruits of technological advance to bear on human needs. Solving social and economic problems called for increasing research and development in both the private and the public sector. The way to ensure that such technologies and solutions were forthcoming would be to construct an educational system for the identification, recruitment, and training of individual talent. Under this guise, equality of opportunity (for improving one's knowledge and skills) was seen as essential for society, because discrimination against those who might someday be society's problem solvers would penalize everyone. Higher education opportunities were seen as particularly crucial for enabling the meritocratic society, since it was in the laboratories and graduate programs of America that research on the new technologies was to occur and solutions to all human problems were to be found.

Not coincidentally, meritocratic theorists accepted the fact that rewards to individuals would be different, based on the technological/scientific contributions each might make toward solving human problems (e.g., energy needs, environmental pollution, more efficient agricultural production, increasing the human lifespan by discovering cures for cancer or diabetes, etc.). Therefore, meritocratic theory as posited by contemporary social scientists gives sociological justification for encouraging both government and individual investment in human capital formation. Meritocratic theory claims that knowledge is the base upon which social progress depends, and that schools are the place for locating those able to contribute to collective life, as well as the most obvious institution for extending our knowledge base.

Even more relevant to contemporary interests in school reform has been the perspective offered by sociologists like Daniel Bell that the future of social and economic progress in the United States lies in our understanding of the coming of post-industrial society. Spokespersons for the significance of the post-industrial age in America argue that our society is in the midst of a cultural and economic revolution that parallels that of the industrial revolution of the last century. The industrial revolution altered the occupational and demographic structure of the nation via technological advances in manufacturing and agriculture. The mechanization of agriculture and industry allowed many Americans to leave their farms and pursue occupations in newly emerging cities. During the nineteenth century, America changed from a rural and agricultural nation to a primarily urban and industrial one. Yet in order to survive and prosper in America's growing workforce, what one needed was a philosophy of hard work, and on-the-job training within a growing manufacturing economy (see Chapters 4 and 5).

The post-industrialists, however, argue that continued advances in technology and factory mechanization are bringing about a revolutionary new society, where new employment growth is occurring only in advanced technological and human service areas. Gone are the days, according to this view, when Americans can get unskilled jobs. Rather, America's future workers must be both highly educated and flexible. Given the rapidly changing technological nature of work, Americans may have to change careers often during their lifetimes as new innovations and inventions make their previous work obsolete. As America's future depends on a well educated and adaptable workforce, extended years of education are seen as desirable, and much of this education ought to be focused on the professional and technical skills required for a post-industrial society.

One of the most important aspects of the post-industrial interpretation of the direction of American society is its acceptance of human capital theory as it relates to the future productivity of the economy. Daniel Bell, for example, combined post-industrial, meritocratic, and human capital themes in his assessment of the future needs of American society:

> The post-industrial society, in its initial logic, is a meritocracy. . . .
> Technical skill, in the post-industrial society, is what the economists call
> "human capital.". . . Differential status and differential income are based
> on technical skills and higher education. Without those achievements one

cannot fulfill the requirements of the new social division of labor which is a feature of that society. And there are few high places open without those skills. To that extent, the post-industrial society differs from society at the turn of the twentieth century. . . . Today, in medicine, law, accounting, and a dozen other professions, one needs a college degree and accrediting, through examination, by legally sanctioned committees of the profession, before one can practice one's art. . . . Within the corporation, as managerial positions have become professionalized, individuals are rarely promoted from shop jobs below but are chosen from the outside, with a college degree as the passport of recognition.[14]

SUMMARY

Economic and social developments in the twentieth century have increasingly brought state and federal governments into economic and educational affairs. Partially informed by Keynesian economics, the government of the United States underwrote many social programs that both provided direct relief to poverty stricken Americans *and* was designed to stimulate the economy. Government involvement in the economy accelerated greatly during the Second World War. By the 1950s and 1960s, the federal government was heavily involved in the economic life of the nation in the areas of monetary policy, of development of the roads, bridges, and dams necessary for transportation and energy systems, and of subsidizing theoretically vital defense and technological needs of the nation.

During the last several decades, state and federal governments have also become increasingly involved in public educational affairs. While public leaders have historically been interested in educating children to fit into and contribute to social progress, only since the 1950s have social scientists and economists linked arms to call for systematic intervention in public school policy. The concept of human capital, which we have been following throughout this book, was first applied seriously during the 1950s and 1960s. Coupled with modernization theory and post-industrial social perspectives, human capital theory has been referred to increasingly to guide educational policy discussions both in the United States and around the world.

On the other hand, human capital theory and related functionalist models from the social sciences received much criticism in the 1960s and 1970s, the content of which will be discussed extensively in Chapters 8 and 9. Among other problems, economists of education are still confronted with major difficulties in attempting to calculate rates of return to the economy for educational institutions that often champion noneconomic goals like enhancement of student self-esteem, valuing knowledge for its own sake, or teaching students to be good citizens. Even so, a combination of factors in the late 1970s and early 1980s brought the perspectives of the economics of education and education as human capital back to the forefront of debates and policy making regarding improvement in public schooling. The reemergence of belief in the utility of human capital theory for current and future school policy making is discussed and a number of specific proposals for making American public schooling more relevant to perceived American economic needs are reviewed in the next chapter.

NOTES

1. Ross Harrold, *The Evolving Economics of Schooling*. Victoria, Australia: Deacon University Press, 1985.
2. Ken Cole, John Cameron, and Chris Edwards, *Why Economists Disagree*. London: Longman Group Ltd., 1983.
3. See, for example, the typologies of John Kenneth Galbraith in *Economics and the Public Purpose*. Boston: Houghton Mifflin, 1973; see also Heilbroner, *The Worldly Philosophers*.
4. Galbraith, *Economics and the Public Purpose,* 1973.
5. Theodore Schultz, "Investment in human capital," *American Economic Review,* 51 (March, 1961): 1–17.
6. Mary Jean Bowman, "The Human Investment Revolution in Economic Thought," *Sociology of Education,* 39 (2), 1966: 111–137; Elchanan Cohn, *The Economics of Education,* Cambridge, MA: Ballinger, 1979; B. F. Kiker, "The Historical Roots of the Concept of Human Capital," *Journal of Political Economy,* 74 (5), 1966: 481–499.
7. Mary Jean Bowman, "Human Investment," p. 114.
8. Mark Blaug, *A Selected Annotated Bibliography in the Economics of Education*. London: University of London, Institute of Education, 1964.
9. Theodore Schultz, *Investing in People: The Economics of Population Quality*. Berkeley, CA: University of California Press, 1981.
10. C. E. Black, *The Dynamics of Modernization*. New York, Harper & Row, 1966, p.7.
11. A. Inkeles and D. Smith, *Becoming Modern: Individual Change in Six Developing Countries*. Cambridge MA: Harvard University Press, 1974, p. 143.
12. J. Atkinson and B. Hoselitz, "Entrepreneurship and personality," in N. and W. Smelser (eds.), *Personality and Social Systems*. New York: Wiley, 1970, p. 534.
13. Robert Dreeben, *On What is Learned in School*. Reading, MA: Addison-Wesley, 1968.
14. Daniel Bell, "On meritocracy and equality," in J. Karabel and A. H. Halsey (eds.), *Power and Ideology in Education*. New York: Oxford University Press, 1977, pp. 607–608.

CHAPTER 7

An Educational Crisis in the 1980s? Economic Development and Educational "Excellence"

As earlier chapters in this book have shown, school reform and educational innovation have been central themes in American history since the middle of the nineteenth century. While it would be a mistake to suggest that all significant efforts to alter educational policy in the United States have stemmed from economic development concerns, it certainly is the case that many American educators have frequently been urged and have been ready to accept school reforms consistent with the perceived needs of the private sector. Increasingly during this century, business leaders, mainstream social scientists, and economists have argued that economic development is synonymous with social progress. And the school has been declared an important basis for both.

In contemplating how our schools have continually been the object of reforms deemed desirable for economic development purposes of the nation, however, we need not always think in the past tense. At this very moment, as outlined in Chapter 1, proposals and policies for reforming American schools so as to make them better meet the needs of the private sector are in full swing. Furthermore, such efforts are currently being pursued at state and federal levels, not just in our local school districts or through professional associations of educators and civic groups. Increasingly, business and political leaders have turned to economists and social scientists for proof that formal schooling is systematically related to economic growth needs of our economy and the economies of other nations around the world. In this chapter, our interest is in elaborating on the economic and educational "crises" of the United States in the late 1970s and early 1980s and in describing how school programs are being developed to better relate the mission of public education to national economic development. Before we investigate this topic, however, a few words about important mid-twentieth-century school reform trends are necessary.

SIGNIFICANT SCHOOL REFORM
EFFORTS FROM THE 1930s TO THE 1970s

From the 1930s to the 1950s, the primary focus of public education continued to be one of improving the process whereby young people could theoretically find their vocational and domestic positions in American life. The secondary school curriculum continued to track students toward future occupational roles, based on the results of "scientifically validated" achievement tests and tests of vocational preference. In addition, a host of new courses became available in high schools designed to give students further practice and training in the "arts" of domestic living. In any event, even during the Depression years Americans continued to believe that public education was increasing in importance for the future of their children and for the future of the nation.[1] (See Figure 7.1 for data on student enrollment.)

Important criticisms of "life adjustment" education were prevalent, however, throughout this period. Advocates for a more academically rigorous liberal arts curriculum, for example, criticized much of the vocational education and home economics emphases in our secondary schools as intellectually vacuous endeavors. Indeed an important social reconstructionist movement developed in the United States between the Great Depression and World War II. Many education professors and school personnel were convinced that the capitalist economic system was seriously flawed and that the schools should provide the vanguard for reconstructing American society. As you may have guessed, educators espousing an anti-business educational curriculum were targeted as public enemies in the late 1940s and 1950s, as tensions with the USSR mounted.[2]

What really undermined life-adjustment education programs in the late 1950s, however, was the "Sputnik" crisis. Specifically, it was claimed the Soviet Union had begun to surpass America technologically. This was demonstrated by the fact that the Russians had put a space satellite into orbit before we did. For our purposes, school reforms following from this "crisis" signified a dramatic new step in linking national interests with schooling. The academic community argued that the future success of the nation depended on the creation and utilization of new scientific knowledge; that advanced knowledge was to be acquired in higher education programs; that life-adjustment programs were not rigorous and challenging enough to prepare future scientific leaders of the nation; and that state and federal governments needed to become involved in school reforms required to advance education

5 and 6 years old

Year	Value
1910	34.6
1920	41.0
1930	43.2
1940	43.0
1950	55.8
1960	63.8
1970	72.4
1980	86.3

7 to 13 years old

Year	Value
1910	86.1
1920	90.6
1930	95.3
1940	95.0
1950	95.7
1960	97.5
1970	97.3
1980	98.8

14 and 15 years old

Year	Value
1910	75.0
1920	79.9
1930	88.8
1940	90.0
1950	93.1
1960	94.1
1970	95.9
1980	97.8

16 and 17 years old

Year	Value
1910	43.1
1920	42.9
1930	57.3
1940	68.7
1950	74.5
1960	80.9
1970	89.3
1980	88.4

18 and 19 years old

Year	Value
1910	18.7
1920	17.8
1930	25.4
1940	28.9
1950	32.3
1960	42.1
1970	56.6
1980	52.3

20 to 24 years old

Year	Value
1910	NA
1920	NA
1930	7.4
1940	6.6
1950	12.9
1960	14.6
1970	21.3
1980	23.5

NOTE:
NA–Data not available.

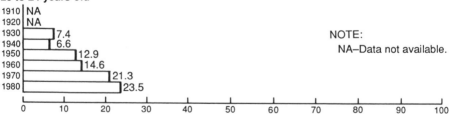

Figure 7.1. Percentage Enrolled in School by Age: 1910–1980. (Source: U.S. Department of Commerce, Bureau of the Census, *Characteristics of the Population: General Social and Economic Characteristics: United States Summary, 1980 Census of Population* [Washington, DC, Supt. of Public Documents, Government Printing Office, 1980].)

in the United States. During the following decade, state and federal governments became heavily involved in setting new academic standards for schools, beefing up the requirements for classroom teachers, providing loans and scholarships for scientific study in colleges and universities, and actually developing and disseminating curricular materials for the teaching of science and math in many local school districts.

By the 1960s and 1970s, a new conventional wisdom had emerged: that *higher* (not just secondary) education was a requirement for occupational success. The private sector continually emphasized how individual standards of living in the nation were dependent on scientific advance. Famous advertising slogans of the day included "better living through chemistry" (for a large chemical company) and "progress is our most important product" (for a prominent household appliance maker). There seemed little dispute among Americans that a college education was desirable, as enrollments in colleges and universities mushroomed, and even a new type of institution for higher education (the community or junior college) was born in many states.

Signifying the continuing belief in the value of education for individual advancement as well as national economic development, two serious social issues of the 1960s and 1970s centered on educational concerns in higher education. One involved equality of educational opportunity. As a college degree continually appeared as a prerequisite for a good job, minority demands for access to existing universities increased, as well as demands for new state institutions closer to where large concentrations of minority students lived. Somewhat later, questions of curricular relevance seemed important to many college students. As more and more students entered universities in the hope of increasing their employment possibilities, they sometimes encountered a university faculty and administration wedded more to liberal arts notions about the purpose of higher education. As you should recognize, the 1960s' and 1970s' issues of equality of educational opportunity and the relevance of occupational training in the schools were already important educational issues 100 years ago. However, even though there existed conflict and controversy about educational curricula and enrollment, rarely did Americans during the 1960s and 1970s question that the primary functions of education involved knowledge acquisition, knowledge generation, and economic development/success.

DISSATISFACTION WITH PUBLIC EDUCATION AND THE EDUCATIONAL EXCELLENCE MOVEMENT

During the past 150 years, school reform efforts have typically followed perceived national crises. We have reviewed throughout this book a number of these ostensible crises, particularly those calling for school reform consistent with national economic development needs. At the time of this writing, we are in the middle of another perceived crisis, where calls and proposals for dramatic school reform efforts are underway. In the late 1980s, the logic and policies that are coming to dominate significant school reform have become couched in the rhetoric of educational excellence. What is particularly compelling about calls to school reform based on such a concept is: how can you argue with anyone who seeks to make schools excellent? And what educator or citizen of the nation would want to go on record as opposing educational excellence?

Not surprisingly, most contemporary calls for school reform have been coupled with arguments that economic development needs of the nation demand a well-educated population and that the crisis of today is that educators have let the nation down in terms of academic standards. Put another way, proposals for improving education today operate under the assumption that developing better human resources for economic development ought to be the primary criterion by which educational excellence is defined. An excellent school is one in which learner outcomes consistent with economic needs of the state and nation can be observed and measured.

PERCEPTIONS OF OUR EDUCATIONAL CRISIS IN THE 1980s

The tone for school reforms consistent with educational excellence was first set by the National Commission on Educational Excellence (NCEE) in 1983. The NCEE was an educational study group comprised primarily of businessmen and senior university officials. According to them, public school performance had sunk to a dismal state, and few if any public schools in the nation could indeed be called adequate, let alone excellent. The very title of the report suggests the seriousness with which this group pursued many of the school reforms we are witnessing today. It was called *A Nation at Risk: The Imperative for Educational Reform*. The language used in the document also suggests the ends to which public education ought to be directed in America (but has not been). According to the panel:

> Our nation is at risk. Our once unchallenged preeminence in commerce, industry, science, and technological innovation is being overtaken by competitors throughout the world. . . . We report to the American people that while we can take justifiable pride in what our schools and colleges have historically accomplished and contributed to the United States and the well-being of its people, the educational foundations of our society are presently being eroded by a rising tide of mediocrity that threatens our very future as a Nation and a people. . . . If an unfriendly foreign power had attempted to impose on America the mediocre educational perfor-

mance that exists today, we might well have viewed it as an act of war. As it stands, we have allowed this to happen to ourselves. . . . We have, in effect, been committing an act of unthinking, unilateral disarmament.[3]

Yet, the NCEE report was but one of literally hundreds of similiar "studies" issued between 1983 and 1987. Another overview of the ostensible crisis in public education, *Making the Grade,* was authored by the prestigious Twentieth Century Fund Task Force on Federal and Secondary Education Policy. This study group described the status of our public schools in these terms:

> The nation's public schools are in trouble. By almost every measure—the commitment and competency of teachers, student test scores, truancy and dropout rates, crime and violence—the performance of our schools falls far short of expectations. To be sure, there are individual schools and school districts with devoted teachers doing a commendable job of educating their students, but too many young people are leaving the schools without acquiring essential learning skills and without self-discipline or purpose.[4]

In another study, the Education Commission of the States (ECS) put forward what they considered a comprehensive plan for improving American schools by the end of the century. Not surprisingly, their analysis also criticized public education of the 1970s and 1980s for what they perceived as gross underdevelopment of human capital resources of the nation. And very importantly, this report (entitled *Action for Excellence*) based calls for school reform explicitly on human capital theory and the research of educational economist Edward Denison. In their report, the Joint Task Force declared:

> It is our conviction that sustained economic growth is essential. And it is our judgment that a high general level of education is perhaps the most important key to economic growth. Common sense compels the conclusion, and observation confirms it, that for any nation, knowledge is power; that trained intelligence is a chief component of individual and national productivity, of a nation's capacity to innovate, and of its general economic health. . . . We have expected too little of our schools over the past two decades, in terms of quality—and we have gotten too little. The result is that our schools are not doing an adequate job of education for today's requirements in the workplace, much less tomorrow's. If we are serious about economic growth in America—about improving productivity; about recapturing competitiveness in our basic industries and maintaining it in our newer industries; about guaranteeing to our children a decent standard of living and a rewarding quality of life, then we must get serious about improving education. And we must start now.[5]

Continuing in the vein of earlier reports, the Carnegie Forum on Education and the Economy also issued a report, entitled *A Nation Prepared: Teachers for the 21st Century,* which dwelled upon the human capital theme. Echoing much of the earlier discussion of this book, the Carnegie Forum described America's previous economic success as a function of the training of students to adjust and fit into the rapidly expanding economy of the first half of the twentieth century:

> This country developed the world's most productive economy in part by mass production techniques that made it possible to employ workers with modest skills to turn out high quality, inexpensive products in great volume. The economic benefits were passed on to workers in the form of rising wages, which they used to create a steadily expanding market for the goods and services they produced. The key was machinery. Very expensive machines were designed so as to reduce to a minimum the skills needed to operate them. . . . This is precisely the area in which we are today being beaten, because the same machinery is now available to others who are willing to work much longer hours than we are, at much lower wages, and markets are no longer national but worldwide.[6]

In order to continue our high standard of living, according to the Carnegie Forum, prevailing notions about the importance of schooling for economic development need to change, and our schools must be restructured to effect such a change:

> In the future, high-wage level societies will be those whose economies are based on the use on a wide scale of very highly skilled workers, backed up by the most advanced technologies available. . . . When [workers] are well educated, they more than pay for their high salaries by adding more to the value of the products they create and the services they offer than less skilled workers can possibly match. Investment in people requires far greater lead time than investment in machinery. Countries that fail to invest enough, or in time, will find the costs—sluggish productivity growth, joblessness, and declining real income—very high.[7]

PROPOSALS TO REMEDY THE "RISING TIDE OF MEDIOCRITY" IN U.S. SCHOOLS

Each of the three reports just mentioned criticizes school leaders and school teachers in the United States for not preparing students properly for the emerging world economic order. Indeed, most currently available reform reports suggest that educational systems in nations challenging us economically are also turning out better educated students (see Table 7.1). If America wants to remain economically competitive, it must use the public schools more effectively for the development of human capital, as do our economic competitors. Therefore, in addition to criticizing schools and those who operate within them, most of the currently available school reform reports propose a variety of ways for schools to become better developers of our human resources (i.e., children).

According to most reform reports, a primary difference between future work in a post-industrial society and what characterized yesterday's occupations has to do with "structural unemployment." As business, economics, and social science experts supposedly confirm:

> The possibility that other nations may outstrip us in inventiveness and productivity is suddenly troubling Americans. Communities all over the United States are depressingly familiar now with what experts call technological, or structural unemployment: Joblessness that occurs because our workers, our factories and our techniques are suddenly obsolete. To many Americans, technological change today seems a dark and threatening force, rather than a bright confirmation of our national genius.[8]

Therefore, and in accord with human capital theory, most reform proposals currently visible argue that more schooling for everyone (not just the technical elite) is an imperative. Rather than preparing students to obtain a job in one company and one industry (as business leaders had hoped young people would do earlier this century), schools are now enjoined to create "flexible" employees who would expect to change careers (and move from town to town) frequently over the course of their employment histories. Yet, merely helping students to "fit in" with changing industrial developments is not the aim of current school reforms. Rather, schools are to train all students to contribute to the expanding knowledge base of our industries. Paradoxically, of course, such contributions may potentially bring about the structural unemployment predicted by post-industrial seers—and may theoretically cost highly educated workers their jobs.

While differences between the four reports just reviewed (and the many others) do exist, some basic agreement on how the schools ought to be reformed is apparent within all of them. Central to most reform themes are renewed emphases on academic standards and achievement expectations. One way to improve academic achievement for all students, promulgated in the reports, is to increase the amount of time students spend on academic materials in the classroom and on their homework. In the typical school day, it is argued, too much time is wasted between classes and too much in-class time seems to be spent doing nonacademic activities. In addition, extracurricular activities like sports and social clubs seem to routinely cut into academic activities, and their impact ought to be minimized. Therefore, most reform proposals have recommended longer school years for students, more class periods during the day, a longer school day, and more effective

TABLE 7.1. AVERAGE PERCENT OF ITEMS ANSWERED CORRECTLY ON AN INTERNATIONAL MATHEMATICS TEST OF 8TH GRADE STUDENTS: SELECTED COUNTRIES, 1981–82

Country or Province	Mean Percentage Correct, All Items[1]	Arithmetic	Algebra	Geometry	Measurement	Statistics
1	2	3	4	5	6	7
Average	*47.4*	*50.5*	*43.1*	*41.4*	*50.8*	*54.7*
Belgium						
Flemish	53.2	58.0	52.9	42.5	58.2	58.2
French	51.4	57.0	49.1	42.8	56.8	52.0
Canada						
British Columbia	51.6	58.0	47.9	42.3	51.9	61.3
Ontario	49.0	54.5	42.0	43.2	50.8	57.0
England and Wales	47.2	48.2	40.1	44.8	48.6	60.2
Finland	46.8	45.5	43.6	43.2	51.3	57.6
France	52.5	57.7	55.0	38.0	59.5	57.4
Hong Kong[2]	49.4	55.1	43.2	42.5	52.6	55.9
Hungary	56.0	56.8	50.4	53.4	62.1	60.4
Israel	45.0	49.9	44.0	35.9	46.4	51.9
Japan[2]	62.1	60.3	60.3	57.6	68.6	70.9
Luxembourg	37.5	45.4	31.2	25.3	50.1	37.3
Netherlands	57.1	59.3	51.3	52.0	61.9	65.9
New Zealand	45.5	45.6	39.4	44.8	45.1	57.3
Nigeria	33.6	40.8	32.4	26.2	30.7	37.0
Scotland	48.4	50.2	42.9	45.5	48.4	59.3
Swaziland	31.5	32.3	25.1	31.1	35.2	36.0
Sweden	41.8	40.6	32.3	39.4	48.7	56.3
Thailand	42.2	43.1	37.7	39.3	48.3	45.3
United States	45.3	51.4	42.1	37.8	40.8	57.7

[1] Weighted average determined by the number of items in each test component.

[2] Students in Japan and Hong Kong were attending the seventh grade.

(*Source: Center for Education Statistics, Digest of Education Statistics, Office of Educational Research and Improvement, U.S. Dept. of Education [Washington, DC: U.S. Government Printing Office, May 1987], p. 303.*)

use of time during the school day. Most of these recommendations have been urged by various study groups because schools in most other industrialized countries already practice them (specifically Japan and West Germany).

Relatedly, the NCEE report and the ECS report each recommend that more and better taught academic subjects should fill the high school curriculum in the United States. They point out and object to the fact that many high school students in the United States routinely get credit toward graduation for such subjects as home economics, typing, and driver's education. Rather, they argue that a more strictly academic curriculum would better prepare future American workers for the rigors of life in the Information Age. All students, they argue, ought to have advanced math and advanced science, and all secondary school students should have systematic exposure to computers and foreign language instruction.

The lower expectations Americans have come to have for educational performance are also visible at home, according to the NCEE and ECS reports. Noting that American students typically have far less homework than do their European counterparts, these panels urged schools and teachers to assign more and demand more time at home be spent on school-related academic activities. In all of the cases suggested above, the common denominator is that the key to a better education and to greater (future) productivity lies in attainment of better academic skills as they have been developed among students. And the quality of such skills is argued to be a function of the amount of time put into acquiring them in school. Thus, the more time devoted to learning academic materials at home and in school, the better educated the student now, and the more economically productive later.

Another ostensible indicator of the current crisis in American education, according to all four panels, is that classroom teachers do not seem either as talented or as well trained as they used to be. Therefore, numerous recommendations were made for improving the training and practice of future classroom instructors. For example, fewer hours in teacher preparation programs ought to be devoted to courses in curriculum methods, and more hours in the teacher's content area ought to be required. In addition, since increasing numbers of those going into teaching are coming from the lowest ability groups in college, better methods of attracting and rewarding future teachers is seen to be important. In particular, all four reports suggest that science and math teachers are increasingly in short supply, and new strategies for getting people interested in teaching such subjects into the schools (and new ways of rewarding them) are crucial.

Another central concern of all reports (except the Carnegie Forum report) is the lack of adequate concentration on academic standards and procedures for assessing them. Specifically, most reports argue that academic requirements in America have been set too low, and that better tests of academic proficiency ought to be developed and utilized. For example, schools should return to an emphasis on grades and grade point averages. Tests used in class to ascertain student performance should be more demanding. Furthermore, a high school diploma ought to be based on a much more extensive academic curriculum, including advanced math and science. And students should be made aware that successful applications to college would be based on how well they performed academically in high school (see Box 7.1).

BOX 7.1   How Will Future Educational Funding Affect Classroom Life?

Funding Linked to "Measurable Outcomes"

By Julie A. Miller

Washington—In keeping with their proclaimed theme for the year, Education Department officials have included in their 1989 budget proposal plans to make schools and colleges more "accountable" for the success of vocational-education and student-aid programs.

"We want to link the level of federal funds a recipient gets to the attainment of measurable outcomes," said a senior e.d. official.

Also tucked away in the budget are plans for a new college-savings program and for overhauling library-aid and immigrant-education programs earmarked for elimination in prior years.

Vocational education, slated for zero funding in 1988, would be level-funded at $888.2 million under the 1989 plan.

But—in a preview of their proposals for next year's reauthorization of the Carl D. Perkins Vocational Education Act—e.d. officials have proposed basing continued funding for local programs on evidence of success.

"Our goal is to improve program quality by strengthening the states' responsibility for setting, assessing, and enforcing standards of performance," said Secretary of Education William J. Bennett.

Department officials said the proposals are modeled after new provisions for the Chapter 1 program, likely to be written into law this year, which would require school districts to improve failing programs.

States would be required to develop evaluation mechanisms—such as basic-skills assessment and placement rates in jobs or postsecondary programs—that measure student achievement. They would have "the authority to determine if programs are working" and the responsibility to step in and aid improvement of those that are not.

Current law requires states to develop measures of program performance, but "gives very little guidance about the kinds of measures the states should develop and contains no requirements about how such measures should be applied," the department's 1989 budget documents state.

"Enactment of these amendments will give the states a mechanism for building strong vocational programs and improving or terminating weak ones."

(Reprinted with permission from Education Week *Vol. 7, No. 21, February 24, 1988.)*

Other prominent themes advanced in many 1980s school reform proposals are calls for more extensive collaboration between the private sector and the public school. Developing school–business partnerships ought to be a major priority of both the school and the private sector, so that the employment and knowledge needs of business can be directly observed by school leaders and students. The Joint Task Force on Education for Economic Growth (the ECS report) put this very succinctly: "If the business community gets more involved in both the design and the delivery of education, we are going to become more competitive as an economy."[9]

WHO SHOULD SPEARHEAD THE REFORMS?

Importantly for themes developed in our earlier chapters, each of the influential reports so far discussed has paid particular attention to whose duty it was to reform the schools. The study commissioned by the federal government (NCEE) argued that the reforms ought to be spearheaded by local and state constituencies, with appropriate guidance and continued (but not necessarily increased) funding by the federal government. The ECS report argued that both national and state economic development goals would be beneficiaries of school reform, and therefore argued that both federal and state agencies ought to "marshall the resources" necessary to improve education. The Twentieth Century Fund, interestingly, declared that much of the problem with contemporary schooling in the United States has been the result of inefficient and muddled priorities on the part of the federal government. In order to make schools excellent, they argued, federal initiatives need better organization and leadership in order for school improvement strategies to be more effectively focused. And finally, the Carnegie Forum report stated that both federal and state authorities needed to take the lead in enhancing educational investments related to improved economic productivity. Yet, since they suggest that an improved educational system will directly increase our gross national product, the Carnegie Forum argues that school improvement will cost nothing extra in the long run. The improvements will in effect pay for themselves through higher economic productivity for the nation.

While a difference of opinion as to who should finance the reforms called for in each of these reports is clearly evident, we can still note that the responsibilities of leadership and the development of strategies for reforming public education are in each case laid at the feet of state and federal experts. An underlying theme of all the reports is that local communities and professional educators have allowed our educational system to become mediocre, because they have not realized that our children are really human resources for state and national economic development. What excellent schools need is effective leadership. Fortunately, according to many reform-minded groups, educational experts are now coming to know "what works" in raising educational achievement levels. And this expertly derived knowledge needs national emphasis and distribution to allow all American schools to become more productive.

TEACHING (NEOCLASSICAL) ECONOMICS IN THE PUBLIC SCHOOL

A final educational need not explicitly addressed in the national school reform reports, yet consistent with their message, is for better understanding among school children of how our economic system works. In order to better convince students about the imperative for economic growth and the importance of the free enterprise system, a number of privately funded organizations have sought to make school children more "economically literate." For example, the Joint Council on Economic Education (located in New York City) helps to fund fifty state councils whose mission is to "improve" economics instruction in public schools. In order to accomplish this, local chapters sponsor economics education workshops for teachers, publish curriculum materials for classroom use, and provide consultation services for teachers interested in incorporating economic literacy materials into their classes. Although the materials these organizations primarily use essentially represent only the theories and perspectives of neoclassical economists, they typically argue that "economics is the common sense of life."

THE HOLMES GROUP PROPOSAL

The four proposals previously reviewed were among literally hundreds of others linking improved schooling in America to our potential for economic recovery. Since many readers of this book are probably currently enrolled in teacher education programs, you would probably be aware that significant reforms in teacher training have been proposed during the past several years not just by "concerned citizen" groups (like the Carnegie Forum), but also by teacher educators in colleges of education. One of these still controversial proposals was put forward by the Holmes Group of prominent teacher-educator institutions in 1986. Agreeing with other reports that the state of public education was mediocre, the Holmes Group sought to reconstruct the training of American teachers by improving the academic qualifications of future educators in the United States.[10]

For example, the Holmes Group agreed with many critics that practicing educators were frequently inadequately prepared in their content areas. They therefore called for colleges of teacher education to stiffen the preprofessional liberal arts and science requirements for prospective teachers before they could become eligible for specialized classroom training. Relatedly, the Holmes Group called for better screening and monitoring of the academic qualifications and performance of prospective teachers before they were graduated from teacher training programs. Important aspects of the stiffening of entrance and performance requirements for future teachers would involve the development and use of objective assessment instruments to test achievement levels of potential classroom instructors.

The Holmes Group not only was interested in reforming the preparation of teachers, but also called for different career patterns for teachers and an expanded role for colleges of education in the evolution of teaching effectiveness. For example, the Holmes Group suggested that teacher preparation programs ought to run like medical training programs, where teachers and university faculty had continuous interaction with one another. Professors ought to go into the schools to observe, teachers ought to continuously return to colleges of education to update their skills (based on the most recent research), and both sets of participants should conduct studies of educational effectiveness for future classroom strategies and efforts.

One of the most controversial suggestions made by the Holmes Group, and supported roundly across the United States by a variety of citizen- and business-dominated advisory commissions (like three of the four reviewed earlier) involved the notion of a career ladder for teachers. Arguing that a better reward structure would improve the status and practice of teaching, the Holmes Group suggested that novice, professional, and lead or master teacher ranks should be instituted in the schools. To go along with such titles, teachers ought to have salary increments consistent with the slightly different duties they would perform (see Box 7.2). Novice teachers, for example, would be new graduates just coming into the profession. Whereas professional teachers would be those who had mastered the characteristics of effective teaching, as judged by administrators and fellow teachers, master teachers would not only have been verified as effective in their classrooms, but would also have additional leadership duties in the school, including the evaluation of novice and professional teachers.

SUMMARY

Theories linking the fate of our nation's economy, the future well-being of our children, and the importance of formal education have come a long way. During the century and a half since the common school began, schools were believed to be necessary for character training and moral development of children. Later, schools were seen as a place where social cohesion and social progress as it related to economic expansion could be facilitated. Throughout this period, and into the 1960s and 1970s, public education was

---

BOX 7.2   A School Reform Strategy Targeted at Classroom Teachers

Reagan Praises Teachers and Incentive Pay

VIENNA, VA.—In a speech at Oakton High School here last week, President Reagan touted the Fairfax County, Va., school system's incentive-based efforts to professionalize teaching and encouraged students to consider entering the field.

"Fairfax County has shown the nation how to upgrade the teaching profession by demonstrating how to attract and retain good teachers," Mr. Reagan said.

"Career ladders, performance-based pay, and other initiatives help to keep good teachers in the profession, and everybody benefits—students, parents, and teachers."

The Fairfax system is phasing in a controversial career-ladder plan that evaluates teachers on a five-point scale. Those who qualify for advancement will begin receiving additional pay during the 1989–90 school year.

The President praised the district's superintendent, Robert R. Spillane, for promoting a plan that "rewards excellence in the teaching profession just as we reward excellence in any other profession."

"We've begun to introduce free-market principles like incentives and accountability to education," the President said.

Mr. Reagan said he hoped that such moves would continue to attract more people to teaching. He cited a recent poll that he said showed "a sharp increase among college students who intend to enter the teaching profession."

When he asked students in the audience who were planning to become teachers to raise their hands, however, only a few responded.

(Reprinted with permission from Education Week, *Vol. 7, No. 27, March 30, 1988.)*

---

seen as a system whereby all citizens could have equal access to the fruits of our ever-increasing economic development. Contrary to much of the conventional wisdom heard in school reform today, most significant school "improvement" efforts in our history have been specifically guided by economic development concerns, broadly defined.

Yet, the predominance of our national economy has recently been challenged (again) by international competition, and American public schools have become targets of business and civic groups interested in more effectively developing our human resources for international competition. And the reforms and policies proposed have had and will continue to have a great impact on what gets taught in our classrooms, who will do the teaching, and how they will be rewarded for their work.

It is to be noted, by the way, that most of the reports criticizing contemporary schooling have themselves been criticized for poor scholarship and inadequate conceptualization. Notably absent from most of the reports are the names of educational historians and sociologists who would be familiar with the emergence and dynamics of public schools in America and in other countries.[11] A variety of economists and social scientists have taken issue with assumptions that educational "mediocrity" in the 1960s and 1970s had anything to do with declining productivity in the United States over the past few years. We will address such concerns in the next two chapters.

Yet, whether the reform reports of the 1980s are true or not is almost a secondary concern here. What is of interest is that increasing numbers of Americans are coming to believe that educational objectives are or ought to be systematically related to the process of economic development. As many contemporary (and historical) critics of capitalism point out, ever-increasing economic development may never solve America's many social problems, as advocates of this theory suggest. It is hardly likely that continually emphasizing the economic benefits of public education for national development will solve problems of inequality and poverty in America and around the world. Yet, touting academic excellence under the guise of developing our human resources reveals an important new rationale linking the purpose of the school with the logic of economic development. As one important critic of this movement notes:

> The major national reports on education in the United States have acted to alter the very discourse of education. They shift the terrain of debate from a more social democratic concern to the language of efficiency, standards, and productivity. . . . The reports and the proposals for "reforming" education that they entail are the result of an accord between right-wing populist groups, capital, and the new middle class. Even though the documents' perspectives on both the economy and schooling are seriously deficient, the reports do succeed in disarticulating many of the dominant themes of the previous social democratic accord. . . . The ultimate effect may be eliminating from our collective memory why inequality in education, the economy, and in politics was [once] of public concern.[12]

NOTES

1. David Tyack, Robert Lowe, and Elizabeth Hansot, *Public Schools in Hard Times: The Great Depression and Recent Years*. Cambridge, MA: Harvard University Press, 1984.
2. Diane Ravitch, *The Troubled Crusade*. New York: Basic Books, 1983.
3. National Commission on Excellence in Education, *A Nation at Risk: The Imperative for Educational Reform*. Washington, DC: U.S. Department of Education, 1983, p. 5.
4. Twentieth Century Task Force on Federal and Secondary Education Policy, *Making the Grade*. New York: The Twentieth Century Fund, 1983, p. 3.
5. Joint Task Force on Education for Economic Growth, *Action for Excellence: A Comprehensive Plan to Improve Our Nation's Schools*. Denver, CO: Education Commission for the States, 1983, p. 18.

6. Carnegie Forum on Education and the Economy, *A Nation Prepared: Teachers for the 21st Century*. New York: Carnegie Forum on Education and the Economy, 1986, pp. 12–13.

7. *Ibid.*, p. 13.

8. The Holmes Group, *Tomorrow's Teachers*. East Lansing, MI: The Holmes Group, 1986.

9. Carnegie Forum, *A Nation Prepared*.

10. Holmes Group, *Tomorrow's Teachers*.

11. See, for example, analyses of these reports by Michael Kirst in *Who Controls Our Schools?* (New York: W.H. Freeman, 1984) and by Lawrence Stedman and Marshall Smith in "Recent Reform Proposals for American Education," *Contemporary Education Review*, 2, 85–104.

12. Michael Apple, "National Reports and the Construction of Inequality," *British Journal of Sociology of Education*, 7 (2), 1986; 171–190.

FOR ADDITIONAL READING

The previously cited works by Diane Ravitch, and Tyack, Lowe, and Hansot give good accounts of school reform and dynamics between the 1930s and 1950s. Joel Spring does a much more thorough job of discussing the 1960s and 1970s in his book *The Sorting Machine* (New York: David McKay, 1976) than I do here. Also, Marvin Lazerson, Judith McLaughlin, and Bruce McPherson talk about the school curriculum of the 1960s and 1970s in "New Curriculum, Old Issues," *Teachers College Record* 86(2), 1984; 299–319.

Not surprisingly, analysis of the logic and the impact of mid-1980s school reform proposals and policies still garners much attention among the ranks of professional educators. The National Governors' Association has published several calls for action on school reform, including their document *Time For Results* (Washington, DC: National Governors' Association, 1986). Meanwhile, a variety of criticisms of such reform proposals are available in the literature. In addition to the Kirst, Stedman and Smith, and Apple works already mentioned, other interesting critiques include Stanley Aronowitz and Henry Giroux's *Education Under Siege* (South Hadley, MA: Bergin and Garvey, 1985); Forrest Keesbury's "Who Wrecked the Schools: Thirty Years of Criticism in Perspective," *Educational Theory*, 34(3) 1984; 209–217; and Madhu Prakash and Leonard Waks' "Four Conceptions of Excellence," *Teachers College Record*, 87(1), 1985; 79–101. Finally, Barbara Finkelstein argues that most of the mid-1980s reform proposals entirely ignore the school's role in helping to build a democratic society in her article "Education and the Retreat from Democracy in the United States, 1979–198?," *Teachers College Record*, 86(2), 1984; 275–282.

CHAPTER 8

Empirical, Theoretical, and Practical Weaknesses in Human Capital Theory

Much contemporary school reform in the United States and around the world specifically links educational dynamics with economic development. And as this logic has continued to intensify throughout the twentieth century, it would appear foolish to suggest that economic utility arguments for public education will diminish in the near future. The growing economic rationale for public education outlined thus far has not been presented in order to defend it, nor necessarily to attack it. My personal bias is that the use of public schooling to prepare students to fit into our prevailing economic system is unfortunate for a variety of reasons (see Chapter 10). Nevertheless, the intent of this book has been to explain the rationale behind historical and contemporary school reform proposals and policies that all students and educators live with daily.

Yet, in order to round out and help bring into focus many of the hidden issues related to education for economic development, some presentation of the weaknesses in the economics of education field (specifically human capital theory) seems well justified. The addition of some critical appraisals related to contemporary school reform based on "children as resources" arguments as well as alternative theoretical positions seems appropriate. Therefore, conceptual and methodological problems with the current "state of the art" in the economics of education (as it relates to school policy) are presented in this chapter. Theoretically critical appraisals of the recent school reform crusade and of human capital theory will be discussed in Chapter 9.

ECONOMIC UTILITY OF PUBLIC SCHOOLING
AS THE CURRENT CONVENTIONAL WISDOM

The field of educational economics has grown rapidly in the United States and around the world during the past several decades. And the economic origins of most contemporary school reform are based now more than ever on arguments that children as human resources are instrumental in the economic development process. Gone even from the rhetoric of school reform so popular today are many of the ostensible goals of education heard just a decade or two ago. Rarely, for example, do we hear from current would-be school reformers the call for "developing the whole child," encouraging within the student a "love for the pursuit of knowledge," or in any broad-based way developing among American children "healthy self-concepts." While the public school's real commitment to any of these objectives has probably always been minimal, many school improvement projects attempted prior to the 1980s usually at least paid lip service to such objectives.

Instead, educational reform proposals and agendas of late have increasingly made specific reference to the economic utility of public education. This process actually began in the 1960s and 1970s, when, as economist Mark Blaug phrased it,

> [the economics of education] was widely acclaimed as opening up new vistas in labor economics, when every discussion of educational planning revolved around the respective merits of the "social-demand approach," the "manpower-requirements approach," and "rate of return analysis." Those were, in short, the "golden years" of the economics of education when no self-respecting minister of education would have dreamed of making educational decisions without an economist sitting at his right hand.[1]

Yet, as Blaug also suggested (and we are about to see), each of these economics-of-education approaches proved to have important limitations.

CONCERNS AND METHODOLOGIES
OF EDUCATIONAL ECONOMISTS

The social demand approach, manpower requirements approach, and rate of return analysis perspectives have all been broadly touched on in preceding chapters. For example, civic demand for educational access has grown throughout the twentieth century in many nations, not just the United States. In many developing countries, growing social demand for the provision of educational opportunity forces policy makers to make choices about where (in the cities vs. in the countryside), for what period of time (elementary education for all vs. only for those able to pursue secondary schooling) and toward which curricular aims (vocational education, basic literacy, scientific/technical training) limited public monies ought to be focused.

In the United States, issues such as how much money ought to be spent and for which levels of schooling have emerged as important concerns over the past several decades. The "social demand" for education in America has made education budgets at local, state, and federal levels one of our biggest public expenditures. Advice is sought from locally available economists regarding capital outlays, bond issues, the question of how much income may be generated by increased property tax assessments, and how best to temporarily invest monies destined for future expenditures. Economists have also frequently been brought in to advise state and federal governments on behalf of various educational groups regarding the economic utility of greater elementary, secondary, and post-secondary educational opportunities.

This latter interest actually relates more specifically to notions about the long-term economic utility of various types of educational programs. In most socialist countries, for example, manpower requirement approaches are used to guide educational planning. If evolving economic opportunities in particular industries are forecast by economists in such nations, programs designed to specifically prepare future workers for those occupations may be designed or added to already existing educational programs. In nonsocialist nations like ours, manpower planning forecasts have been used in two different ways. For example, federal and state governments during the past several decades have appropriated money for establishing new programs and providing educational scholarships in occupational growth areas deemed important for economic growth (see Chapter 6). Moreover, forecasts of emerging occupational needs are typically released by the government to local and state agencies, in the hope that they may enhance or extinguish educational programs linked with either growing or declining industries.

Nationally available forecasts of the requirements for new teachers, for example, are typically referred to by college administrators interested in long-term programming for teacher training programs. As the previous chapter suggests, the current school reform movement has brought about increased concern for more and better trained math and science teachers at the secondary level. In point of fact, advertised vacancies for secondary math and science teachers have increased significantly during the past several years, and labor economists have forecast this area as one of rapid growth for the next decade. Furthermore, such trends and the nationally perceived need for better science and math instruction for economic development purposes have drawn the attention of various public and private (philanthropic) educational groups. And, based on such manpower requirement trends, a variety of loans and scholarships for math and science teachers (as opposed, for instance, to social studies teachers) are available. In other words, even in this country, forecasts of growth in certain occupational areas by economists frequently lead to policies altering the structure of educational opportunities.

RATE OF RETURN ANALYSES
AND HUMAN CAPITAL THEORY

Rate of return analyses, on the other hand, focus less on projections of future job trends, and more on past and current returns to individuals as a function of their educational training (see Table 8.1). Such analyses, popular among human capital economists, hypothesize that individual investments in formal schooling have both individual and systemwide utility. Individual decisions by workers and students to forgo immediate employment in order to obtain further schooling theoretically yield a greater payoff later on. In a sense, investing in one's future earning capabilities (instead of working in the present) is much like the process an industrialist might use in investing in new machinery or other forms of physical capital. Investments in physical capital now will theoretically yield greater plant productivity down the road. Obtaining more or better occupational skills now rather than working will yield more productive (and therefore more remunerative) work down the road. In both cases—for those who invest in physical capital and for those who invest in their own human capital—higher productivity will yield a greater rate of return.

To briefly tie all of this back into the concerns of the previous chapter, remember that the primary objective of the current educational excellence movement is to enhance the individual skills of future workers. That is, the claim is made that more and better schooling will make future workers more productive. Therefore investing now in more technologically productive schooling will enable both students and the larger national economy to be more productive in the long run.

Attempts to verify human capital theory, on which much of the current reform efforts have been based, have led to the use of a variety of rate of return approaches to test the human capital model. One basic economics of education text classifies these analyses into four different types: the *relationship analysis approach;* the *cash value approach;* the *cost benefit approach;* and the *residual approach.*[2]

The *relationship analysis approach* and the *cash value approach* both attempt to compare differences between large numbers of individuals with differing levels of formal schooling. For example, individuals with higher levels of education typically have higher status jobs. University professors, doctors, and lawyers typically have more years of formal education than do grocery clerks, secretaries, or sales personnel at the local department store. So, too, the greater the amount of formal schooling an individual has, the higher the yearly salary and lifetime earnings tend to be.

Frequently, those interested in more refined assessments of the rate of return one may expect by staying in school longer use a *cost benefit approach.* Such an analysis extends the cash value approach by also attempting to quantify how much financial cost is involved in extended educational preparation programs. Importantly, economists using this methodology attempt to include actual costs for school expenses incurred by individuals in attending school, as well as "opportunity costs," or how much income a person must typically forgo in order to pursue additional years of schooling. Again, on average, when one subtracts the costs of extended educational training from the returns in later employment years, it frequently takes several years' worth of one's lifetime earnings to at least compensate for costs of obtaining additional schooling.

Yet, none of the preceding approaches is particularly new in the field of educational economics. We have seen that such methods were used historically by economists in the nineteenth and early twentieth centuries for actuarial purposes; none of them speaks directly to possibilities for enhancing national economic development via public education. On the other hand, the *residual approach,* made famous by such human capital theorists as Theodore Schultz, Gary Becker, and Edward Denison, has been utilized to make the claim that investments in public schooling are systematically linked to national economic productivity and economic growth. Using this method, economists interested in explaining the process of economic growth among Western nations during the twentieth century have typically plotted all commonly agreed upon factors (physical capital, labor costs, and rent) predicting national productivity curves.

Not surprisingly, all of the variability in economic productivity has not been accounted for in such projections. There are just too many factors involved to pin down every possible event or policy related to changes in economic development. Of even more concern to some economists during the twentieth century was that the residual (or unexplained) amount of economic productivity seemed to be growing in Western nations during the century. Some factor systematically related to economic growth therefore had to be influencing this process, but was not being assessed in standard econometric models.

According to human capital theorists, the explanation of a large part of the residual variance in economic growth lay in the increasing skill base of workers within modern economies. More highly skilled workers were more productive workers, the argument ran, and since entering workers were more highly educated than their predecessors, their enhanced skill levels

TABLE 8.1 MEDIAN ANNUAL INCOME OF YEAR-ROUND FULL-TIME WORKERS 25 YEARS OLD AND OVER, BY YEARS OF SCHOOL COMPLETED AND SEX: UNITED STATES, 1970 TO 1985

		Elementary School		High School		College		
		Less than						
Sex and Year	Total	8 years	8 years	1 to 3 years	4 years	1 to 3 years	4 years	5 years or more
1	2	3	4	5	6	7	8	9
Men								
1970	$9,521	$6,043	$7,535	$8,514	$9,567	$11,183	$13,264	$14,747
1971	10,038	6,310	7,838	8,945	9,996	11,701	13,730	15,300
1972	11,148	7,042	8,636	9,462	11,073	12,428	14,879	16,877
1973	12,088	7,521	9,406	10,401	12,017	13,090	15,503	17,726
1974	12,786	7,912	9,891	11,225	12,642	13,718	16,240	18,214
1975	13,821	8,647	10,600	11,511	13,542	14,989	17,477	19,658
1976	14,732	8,991	11,312	12,301	14,295	15,514	18,236	20,597
1977	15,726	9,419	12,083	13,120	15,434	16,235	19,603	21,941
1978	16,882	10,474	12,965	14,199	16,396	17,411	20,941	23,578
1979	18,711	10,993	14,454	15,198	18,100	19,367	22,406	25,860
1980	20,297	11,753	14,674	16,101	19,469	20,909	24,311	27,690
1981	21,689	12,866	16,084	16,938	20,598	22,565	26,394	30,434
1982	22,857	12,386	16,376	17,496	21,344	23,633	28,030	32,325
1983	23,891	14,093	16,438	17,685	21,823	24,613	29,892	34,643
1984	25,497	14,624	16,812	19,120	23,269	25,831	31,487	36,836
1985	26,365	14,766	18,645	18,881	23,853	26,960	32,822	39,335

Women

Year								
1970	5,616	3,798	4,181	4,655	5,580	6,604	8,156	9,581
1971	5,872	3,946	4,400	4,889	5,808	6,815	8,451	10,581
1972	6,331	4,221	4,784	5,253	6,166	7,020	8,736	11,036
1973	6,791	4,369	5,135	5,513	6,623	7,593	9,057	11,340
1974	7,370	5,022	5,606	5,919	7,150	8,072	9,523	11,790
1975	8,117	5,109	5,691	6,355	7,777	9,126	10,349	13,138
1976	8,728	5,644	6,433	6,800	8,377	9,475	11,010	13,569
1977	9,257	6,074	6,564	7,387	8,894	10,157	11,605	14,338
1978	10,121	6,648	7,489	7,996	9,769	10,634	12,347	15,310
1979	11,071	7,414	7,788	8,555	10,513	11,854	13,441	16,693
1980	12,156	7,742	8,857	9,676	11,537	12,954	15,143	18,100
1981	13,259	8,419	9,723	10,043	12,332	14,343	16,322	20,148
1982	14,477	8,424	10,112	10,661	13,240	15,594	17,405	21,449
1983	15,292	9,385	10,337	11,131	13,787	16,536	18,452	22,877
1984	16,169	9,828	10,848	11,843	14,569	17,007	20,257	25,076
1985	17,124	9,736	11,377	11,836	15,481	17,989	21,389	25,928

(Source: Center for Education Statistics, Digest of Education Statistics, Office of Educational Research and Improvement, U.S. Dept. of Education [Washington, DC: U.S. Government Printing Office, May 1987], p. 288.)

must be attributable to their advanced years of education. And this fact, in turn, must account for the increases in economic productivity of the United States and other advanced nations.

The residual approach was made famous by a number of human capital theorists in the 1960s. Theodore Schultz, for example, calculated the increase in educational attainment for all Americans between 1900 and 1957.[3] He then derived a dollar figure to represent how much our "education stock" had increased between the years from 1929 to 1957. Following this, Schultz calculated the residual or unexplained increase in the returns to worker wages during this period and found that workers had increased them by $71 billion over that which could be explained by other economic factors. Correlating increases in labor earnings with increases in educational attainment over this period, he then argued that 44 percent of the increases in workers' wages had been the result of better work for better pay and that this better work had to have come about through more and better educational attainment.

Edward Denison attempted an even more comprehensive study of the growth rate for the United States from 1929 to 1969 using the residual approach. In his study, Denison categorized workers based upon the years of formal education they had received. Subsequently, he calculated both the changes in his index of different types of educated workers and increases in wage rates of the economy. Not surprisingly, Denison found great increases in wage rates over the forty-year period and different change rates among the seven categories of educated labor. According to his figures, wage rates paid to more highly educated labor increased more dramatically than increases to those with less education, and over 27 percent of the aggregate increase in national income was explained by the educational upgrading of the total U.S. workforce.[4]

HUMAN CAPITAL THEORY AND CONTEMPORARY SCHOOL REFORM

The emphasis human capital theory has placed upon the productive (as opposed to consumptive) utility of public schooling for teaching occupational and technological skills, combined with statistical assessments of the contribution of education to economic growth during the middle of this century, enabled those seeking to enhance economic productivity in the 1960s and 1970s to focus on the potential public schools might have in this process. Yet, falling economic productivity curves in the United States during the 1970s and 1980s, coupled with increasing educational attainments (in terms of years of schooling completed) of students, led to three possible conclusions: that human capital theory was seriously flawed (as we will see); that only by enhancing private education could our society guarantee educational excellence; or that public school reform (or restructuring) along lines suggested by our economic competitors needed to be achieved. Some educational economists did in fact begin to doubt important aspects of human capital theory. Other economists and business leaders called for such things as tuition tax credits and educational vouchers to help restore competitiveness in the education "market" (see Chapter 9). However, as Chapter 7 suggests, other economists and many business and policy leaders chose the latter alternative.

METHODOLOGICAL AND THEORETICAL WEAKNESSES IN HUMAN CAPITAL THEORY

While it *may* be true that modern economies depend on the enhanced skills of their workers; while it *may* be true that schools have a role in enhancing worker skills; and while it appears to be true that mainstream social and economic scientists have supported such lines of thought throughout the nineteenth and twentieth centuries, there are those who currently disagree with such statements of "fact" (just as such "facts" were disagreed with earlier). Importantly, while many economists and social scientists still do believe in the modernizing and human capital formation functions of public schooling, others do not. Most economists today probably would acknowledge that aggregate skill levels of a given workforce are related to economic productivity. On the other hand, many are concerned about the relatively unsophisticated calculations of human capital contributions to economic productivity seen in the human capital literature.

As discussed in Chapter 6, economists have traditionally studied the value of human capital both for individuals and for national economies. For individuals, investments in human capital are thought to enhance future earnings potential. Such earnings have then typically been calculated by rate of return analyses, using national census data. Comparing wages of workers with different levels of education clearly shows that workers with different amounts of education have, on average, different wage rates. And many contemporary school reform advocates have used this information to argue for increased educational completion rates for all Americans. However, there is a logical inconsistency in urging everyone to complete high school or college when earnings differences between occupational classifications may be based on educational status. Proponents, in other words, assume that everyone's earnings will go up with more years of education. Actually, as observers like Thomas Green suggest, an inflation in educational credentials is just as likely to bring *down* the economic value of a high school or college diploma. For example, forty or fifty years ago, holders of high school diplomas were among the top income earners in the United States. Now that most Americans have high school diplomas, they command less (relative) return and prestige than they once did. With an overall inflation in educational attainment, obtaining a high school diploma (for example) *may* help one *retain* current economic standards of living (standards once requiring no high school education). But since more people are now obtaining advanced educational credentials, it appears unlikely that obtaining a high school degree will help close the gap *between* classes of differentially educated workers. According to Green, for example, obtaining a high school diploma now is an imperative, not to *improve* one's economic position, but merely to *survive* the onslaught of continuing educational inflation.[5]

Indeed, even within various rate of return analyses there are vast differences between and among classes of educated workers. For example, in the United States we note that returns on educational investments have typically been lower for women and minorities (see Table 8.1). We also note that returns on the educational investment a teacher makes seem to be far less than those received by someone going into business. Somehow, even if skill levels are being enhanced by formal school attendance (which is disputed by many), other factors seem to play a significant role in returns to educational investment. Yet, human capital economists have yet to convincingly disentangle the multiple factors that seem to comprise differential wage rates for employees in capitalist countries. Not knowing exactly how to determine the relative contribution of education toward observed differences within classes of similarly educated workers, economists have typically assigned mathematical weights or percentages to their calculations. According to educational economists like Steve Klees, however, such percentages may give the appearance of sound scientific practice, but are in essence educated guesses. In other words, most rate of return analyses contain an important element of guesswork and are therefore not as methodologically rigorous as they might appear:

> Since their initiation, rate of return to education studies have often estimated the benefits (and opportunity costs) of education by using national census data that summarize wage differences between groups with different levels of educational attainment. However, even initially, it was recognized that the differences between the earnings of groups with different schooling could have been caused by a variety of factors other than education. . . . Astonishingly enough in retrospect, these economists solved the problem by apparently arbitrarily selecting a correction factor, usually set as .6, which meant that 60 percent of the earnings differences associated with educational differences were assumed to be caused by education, and then using this adjusted data to calculate RORs. . . . [these methods] are such obviously inadequate procedures to any researcher that it is surprising that economists still get away with doing so.[6]

Similar scientific deficiencies are demonstrated by human capital researchers seeking to explain the productive value of formal education to national income figures like gross national product. Again, correlational analyses have typically been employed in such studies. Unfortunately, correlational studies are frequently viewed with suspicion by more rigorous academics, especially if cause and effect explanations are the object of the research. Some argue, for example, that economic growth may have preceded increases in educational attainment rates during the twentieth century. For example, rising wage rates (for whatever unknown reason) might just as easily have led to workers keeping their children in school longer than they would have had incomes been smaller. Or, perhaps some other yet-to-be-discovered factor caused increases in both economic productivity *and* educational attainment. In other words, statistical analyses typically used in human capital research (i.e., using residual scores and correlational analyses) have been frequently criticized as exploratory in nature, rather than definitive. But to assume that such correlations tell the whole story, or explain the relationship between variables, is scientifically suspect at best.

THEORETICAL WEAKNESSES
OF HUMAN CAPITAL RESEARCH

On another front, the familiarity of economists with the content and dynamics of public education during this century seems to be lacking, judging by their writings on the subject. As we discussed, human capital economists have traditionally calculated correlation coefficients between years of schooling completed and economic productivity "residuals" over long time spans in the United States and abroad. Yet, we also observed that economists have rarely concerned themselves with the formal school curriculum prior to the last decade or two. Given this reluctance, it seems quite interesting that they are willing to assume productive skills have in some way been transmitted by the school, particularly when at various times during the past forty years schools have been criticized by conservative forces to be too academically soft or focused too much on "life-adjustment" (i.e., nonproductive) activities.

None of the classic studies linking increased economic productivity with years of formal education has attempted to differentiate among the very different types of schooling American adolescents have completed during the twentieth century. Since the studies we have yield no sophisticated econometric data on return to GNP from different types of formal education, how do we scientifically know whether worker productivity during the twentieth century was better facilitated by the different curricular tracks that

American students were placed in during this period? Did children who received more mathematics training earlier in this century contribute more to economic development of the nation than those who studied to be gardeners or art historians? If so, what exactly was the statistical impact of an extra year of mathematics instruction on national economic productivity and returns on individual investment over and above an extra year in the study of soil chemistry or Renaissance painting? If we cannot scientifically answer questions like these, how can we know whether stiffening the current academic requirements of American schools will contribute to greater economic gains in our future "post-industrial" society? In theory this might be the case; it certainly sounds plausible. But we don't have any such proof from economic science.

While these examples may seem rather simplistic, in fact they are not. Remember that many school reformers by the 1950s were claiming that high school education had become trivialized throughout the twentieth century by progressive educators and that few academic skills were being emphasized in the school. Human capital theorists, however, have argued just the reverse: their calculations suggested that economic productivity greatly increased during this period, and they argued that the school must have been responsible.

Perhaps it was the attitude toward work cultivated by the school that made workers very productive later on. Perhaps the lesser emphasis on seatwork and classwork in many progressive schools, combined with more hands-on experience through industrial, vocational, and agricultural education projects, was responsible for this productivity. Perhaps school counselors who efficiently (if inequitably) helped students find suitable employment opportunities prior to the current era were responsible for increased worker productivity. In other words, extra years of education might very well have been related to higher levels of GNP throughout the twentieth century; but it may have had very little to do with the formal academic curriculum of the schools. The truth is we just do not know. And human capital theorists and researchers have yet to demonstrate that they know either. Economist Jesse Burkhead comments:

> The incongruity is that although research on the macroeconomics of education has made important, if perhaps somewhat overrated contributions, research on the microeconomics of education has yielded almost nothing but negative results. If we accept, as seems indisputable, the proposition that investment in education is "productive" for society as a whole, then it should be possible to apply microanalytic techniques to discover those combinations of resources, decision structures, or educational practices that are more productive or less productive of specific outcomes. Unhappily, to date, it hasn't worked. Formal schooling is not all of education, to be sure, but it is an important part of it. The efforts to

analyze schooling as a system have not, as yet, been useful for policy purposes.[7]

Another prominent economist, Lester Thurow, launched a devastating criticism of both the methodological and the theoretical utility of human capital theory during the same years when school reform reports were extolling its virtues. As most human capital theorists will admit, on-the-job training is a primary location for the development of occupational skills (a fact itself rarely referred to by contemporary school reformers). Job-related training in the workforce is supposedly paid for by the worker, as he or she obtains lower than market wages while being "educated." However, while human capital theorists believe that such training can be statistically separated and explained apart from the effects of formal education, economists like Thurow disagree. Thurow offered this assessment of human capital economics:

> Human-capital predictions—the relationship between education and earnings—have been far off the mark. And if you want to understand the dominant mode of acquiring human capital, on-the-job training, the human-capital economics does a disappearing act. . . . For human-capital economists, the predominant on-the-job form of training is made into a market phenomenon by asserting that individuals buy training from their employers by working for less than their market wage . . . if training occurs on the job, it is [difficult] to pin down how much training is going on. There is nothing here that can be called equivalent to a year of education not to speak of a direct measure of the skills acquired. In other words, neither the costs nor the benefits of the most significant way human skills are acquired in our economy can be stated in precise numbers.[8]

Box 8.1 further examines the better skills/better jobs theory.

BOX 8.1   Do More Skills Mean Better Jobs? Not According to This Analysis

Some Economists Question Paranoia about Inflation

Associated Press

NEW YORK—Inflation paranoia has gripped the financial markets, which only a few months back were preoccupied with the threat of a recession. But some economists say the specter of rising prices is highly exaggerated.

These economists argue that unlike in the 1970s, when price spirals became ingrained, the economy of the 1980s has been reshaped by fundamental changes that have restrained costs and wages, two key components of inflation.

Moreover, their reasoning goes, the highly competitive global economy and higher U.S. productivity provide compelling evidence that acute inflation will not revisit the United States soon.

"There's a very slow learning process in the markets," said John Hekman, senior economist at the Claremont Economics Institute, a forecasting firm in Claremont, Calif., that rejects the prevalent thinking about inflation fear. "We've had inflation scares every year."

Unfounded or not, this anxiety has helped wrench down stock and bond prices and raise long-term Treasury yields to the highest levels of 1988. The Federal Reserve has been maneuvering to tighten credit as a pre-emptive step to thwart inflation, and on Wednesday banks responded by raising their prime lending rates.

To some degree, economists said, inflation anxiety results from the stock market crash seven months ago. After the collapse the Fed used a mix of confidence-building public statements and big injections of money into the banking system to quell fears that a recession loomed.

Since then the economy has shown surprising strength, but the uncertainty raised by the crash has lingered. Many investors now say they fear a rapidly expanding economy, because it would mean higher wages, more demand for credit and too much money chasing too few goods. That translates into inflation.

The economists who dispute that view argue that wages have not risen, despite the lowest unemployment in 14 years. On the contrary, wages have fallen in some areas relative to inflation, which last year totaled 4.4 percent and for the first three months of this year ran at an annual rate of 4.2 percent.

"Labor costs have remained meek and mild," said Richard Belous, a labor economist at the Conference Board, a business-financed economic research group in New York. "If inflationary costs start getting imbedded in labor costs, then the ball game's over, but I don't think it's happening."

The primary reason for this, Belous and others said, is that the labor market is radically different now. Many companies have restructured into smaller, leaner operations with non-union workers. Moreover, many Americans are employed in temporary and part-time jobs that offer relatively low wages, little job security and often no benefits.

Management is now playing hardball with labor," Belous said." It can't just pass costs on to the consumer. Markets are deregulated; there's more competiton. We're part of a global economy."

Richard Rahn, economist at the U.S. Chamber of Commerce in Washington, argues that inflation worriers are using outdated economic formulas for assuming that lower unemployment translates into rising prices.

(*Reprinted from the* Lexington Herald Leader, *May 13, 1988, with the permission of the Associated Press.*)

PRACTICAL LIMITATIONS OF APPLIED HUMAN CAPITAL THEORY

Human capital proponents have had their best chance to prove the utility of their theories for the economic development process in less developed countries in the 1960s and the 1970s. Educational economists who came to advise on the institutionalization of education in places without long traditions of public schooling favored several different approaches, yet most of their intervention strategies met with what educational economist George Psacharopoulos of the World Bank termed "planning mishaps." For example, an early mistake educational policy advisors made in developing countries involved the level of education deemed worthy of investment. Economists assumed, for example, that investment in higher education would have greater productivity potential than in early education. In retrospect, they found this was wrong. Either graduates of colleges and universities frequently emigrated to other countries where their talents could be put to better use than at home, or college degrees became a new status symbol for young members of already elite families. In either event, such investments seemed to have little payoff for economic development.

In several countries, vocational schools were instituted on the advice of educational economists who argued that a more practical education would be better for domestic development than general or academic instruction; such schools were quite popular in both South America and Africa. However, follow-up analysis of graduates from such schools frequently found them changing from academic areas in which they were trained into educational programs of very different types. In some instances this finding seemed to be due to lack of job opportunities in the students' chosen field; in other cases students developed higher aspirations than could be achieved through vocational and occupational job placements.

While economists of education still advise and perform research in developing countries on desirable relationships between educational investment and economic productivity, the large-scale policy proposals made by human capital economists have been at best disappointing. Psacharopoulos, himself an advocate for using research from the economics of education in the economic development process, currently claims that educational economists must redefine their role in macroplanning policy for developing countries. After summarizing the poor track record of educational economists in designing economically helpful educational systems around the world, he suggests in what ways they might be useful:

> The foregoing discusion leads to some general principles that the educational planner could confidently consider in shaping future policies: a) gradually reduce government involvement in education; b) pay increased attention to the private (social) demand for education; c) be less concerned with macroplanning models; and d) focus attention on narrower policies to address particular issues.[9]

SUMMARY

While the economics of education has emerged as an important academic discipline during the past thirty years, many economists still view its practical utility with some caution. Educational economists have had less than spectacular success in forecasting employment trends in the late twentieth century; they have published little on the content and dynamics of American education as such factors may have influenced American economic development; they use a combination of sophisticated techniques and educated guesswork to explain rates of return on educational investments; and serious disagreements regarding methods and implications of work in this field are quite apparent among educational economists. In other words, a careful reading of the economics of education literature yields both interesting and informative perspectives. Yet, the fact that this field is still in its academic infancy, characterized by very visible disputes and discrepancies among educational economists, renders policy implications from research in this field rather suspect.

However, the conventional wisdom in the United States and abroad has adopted the concept that education is related to economic development, and this same conventional wisdom views economic development as essential to continued prosperity and social progress in capitalist nations. Therefore, it ought to come as no major surprise that school reformers of the day have latched on to tentative, incomplete, and arguable findings in the economics of education literature to support their continued efforts to make schools better conform to perceived needs of the economic system. In order to get some alternative contemporary perspectives to the conventional wisdom on such matters, we turn to Chapter 9.

NOTES

1. Mark Blaug, "Where Are We Now in the Economics of Education?" *Economics of Education Review*, 4 (1), 1985: 17–28.
2. Roe Johns, Edgar Morphet, and Kern Alexander, *The Economics and Financing of Education*. Englewood Cliffs, NJ: Prentice-Hall, 1983.
3. Theodore Schultz, *The Economic Value of Education*. New York: Columbia University Press, 1963.
4. Edward Denison, *Accounting for United States Economic Growth, 1929–1969*. Washington, DC: Brookings Institution, 1974.
5. Thomas Green, *Predicting the Behavior of the Educational System*. Syracuse, NY: Syracuse University Press, 1980.
6. Steven J. Klees, "Planning and Policy Analysis in Education: What Can Economics Tell Us?" *Comparative Education Review*, 30 (4), November 1986: 574–607.
7. Jesse Burkhead, "Economics Against Education," *Teachers College Board*, 75 (2), 1973: 193–205.
8. Lester Thurow, *Dangerous Currents*. New York: Random House, 1983.
9. George Psacharopoulos, "The Planning of Education: Where Do We Stand," *Comparative Education Review*, 30 (4), November 1986: 560–573.

CHAPTER 9

Theoretical Critiques of Human Capital Theory and Recent School Reform Proposals

In Chapter 8, our focus was on methodological, conceptual, and practical issues and problems with human capital theory as this modern-day economic perspective has been used to justify current school reform efforts. In this chapter, a host of alternative theoretical explanations of the relationship between education and economic development is our concern. Many of the late twentieth-century arguments challenging the logic of using public schools for economic development purposes have their roots in those critical appraisals discussed particularly in Chapters 2 and 4.

NEOCLASSICAL OBJECTIONS TO USING PUBLIC EDUCATION FOR ECONOMIC DEVELOPMENT PURPOSES

As suggested in Chapter 8, many of the methodological concerns regarding the validity of human capital economics come not from radical economists or conflict social scientists, but from other well respected mainstream economists. Importantly, many of these economists are also critical of key theoretical aspects of human capital theory. For example, there remains a healthy conviction among many neoclassical economists that public schools are and by definition will remain inefficient places to teach occupational skills. As public bureaucracies, the argument runs, schools are structured too inefficiently to produce the kinds of skills that specific consumers (like parents or industry) might like. According to them, entrenched bureaucracies, like those found in public education, are not subject to market forces as are organizations in the private sector, and no amount of tinkering with them is likely to totally satisfy consumer (i.e., parent) preferences. For many neoclassical economists, in other words, private schooling (perhaps subsidized by government "vouchers") is the only solution to "improving" education for any purpose, if such improvements are called for by consumers or those in the private sector.

HIGHER EDUCATION AND THE DEVELOPMENT OF HUMAN RESOURCES

In addition to general skepticism among neoclassical economists regarding the efficiency of public institutions to meet consumer demands of specific interest groups in the private sector, more focused theoretical disputes exist regarding the importance of skill acquisition in schools for productive use in the economy. Criticism of the productive utility of higher education has been a favorite target of various economists and social scientists. Significantly, higher education institutions have been touted by human capital theorists and post-industrialist social scientists as central to the technological advance of our culture. Yet, vocationally speaking, such institutions may be the most occupationally inefficient schools within the United States. As discussed earlier, the liberal arts/nonvocational interest of many colleges and college educators is frequently featured or at least acknowledged. Having inherited notions of formal education from classical sources, many universities still claim that Western culture and literature are its main traditions. Paradoxically, the institutions least interested in teaching occupationally relevant skills, and those that are the most expensive to attend (like small liberal arts colleges), are the ones whose graduates earn the highest incomes upon graduation.

Sympathizers with human capital orientations contend that a good liberal arts education teaches one to be a critical thinker and to be occupationally adaptable throughout one's working years. A good liberal arts education helps to prepare one better for the academic and scientific rigors of post-baccalaureate education. However, several different interpretations of the use of higher education for occupational placement have been offered (see Box 9.1).

Some critics of the argument that the function of higher education is to enhance the human resources of young Americans focus on the value of credentials and diplomas independent of years of education and/or skills attained in school. For example, college graduates typically have a significantly greater rate of return on their educational investments than those completing an equivalent number of years of education, yet never receiving a formal degree. Were skill levels relevant to economic productivity the sole criteria for individual success, they argue, such findings should not exist. A

BOX 9.1 **Might Too Much (Higher) Education Be Counter-Productive for Developing Some Worker Skills?**

The Continuing Need for Vocational Education

By Frederick G. Welch

When you walk into a mechanic's garage, do you want to talk about Plato or Charles Dickens? More likely, you want to discuss fuel injection or automatic transmissions.

But if schools follow the "ideal" curriculum recently outlined by U.S. Secretary of Education William J. Bennett—or similar programs proposed by other reformers—you may find that your mechanic is better prepared to identify the *Republic* than he is your radiator.

In promoting an agenda biased toward college-bound students, Mr. Bennett and like-minded critics of American schools ignore the needs of vocational-education students.

The Secretary's hypothetical "James Madison High School," for example, would stress academic toughness in a curriculum centered on the study of Western culture. Course requirements would include four years of English, three years each of science, mathematics, and social studies, and two years of a foreign language.

Such a program would not be appropriate for vocational-education students, who make up a large portion of the high-school population in many communities. As the future workforce for America's industries, these young people deserve an education suited to their interests and goals.

Not all students are cut out for college; some prefer to learn a trade and enter the working world. If we try to force these students into an academic mold, they are likely to become frustrated and drop out of high school.

Certainly all young people should master in school the skills and concepts essential to productive citizenship. They should understand, for instance, the principles of American democracy and economics.

Through practice in reading, writing, speaking, and listening, they must learn to communicate effectively. And they should develop in school the analytical skills necessary to diagnose problems and make decisions based on sound reasoning.

But is it a disaster that every student does not know who Plato was? Do all high-school students need to know every famous author in world literature or each great composer in music history?

Mr. Bennett's curriculum pushes vocational education—what he calls "shop"—into the elective category. Yet it is the technical skills learned in "shop" that will be most important for many students after high-school graduation.

Local factory managers may be impressed by job applicants who can quote Shakespeare, but will they hire them? In real life, supervisors want people with technical skills or work experience.

In their efforts to provide students with the necessary skills, vocational-education programs are currently in the throes of change. Industry is moving from low to high technology. For virtually all vocational fields, computer literacy has become critical. In addressing such developments, combined and upgraded vocational curricula are demanding more of students.

For example, as more cars are constructed with computer systems, auto mechanics must understand microcomputer electronics.

Factory workers need to know more about robotics and microprocessors as more advanced equipment is installed by manufacturers. Cabinetmaking, for instance, while once identified with craftsmanship, now is dominated by computer-driven machines.

At a recent meeting of the World Congress on Vocational Education, held in Australia, representatives of corporations like General Motors and the Volvo Company of Sweden emphasized the need for a broader, multi-craft training for vocational students. To maintain quality while remaining competitive, such companies seek not technical specialists but versatile workers who can manage a cluster of skills.

Hoping to meet this need, many vocational programs are combining courses. Classes in, say, electronics, plumbing, and carpentry may be integrated into building trades. In the past—and sometimes the present—the installation of a light-switch required three workers and six hours of labor: a carpenter to cut a hole, an electrician to run the wire, and a plasterer to patch the hole. From the new perspective, it's a two-hour job for one skilled journeyman.

In light of the ongoing changes in the workplace, schools must also carefully design academic programs for vocational students.

Mathematics, science, and civics should be taught in more practical—but not easier—ways. All vocational-education courses should become more rigorous and more relevant to students' future needs.

The watered-down versions of college-preparatory courses commonly offered to vocational students serve no useful purpose. While such courses approach information abstractly, vocational-education programs should present similar material in applied terms.

A student in an electronics or welding program, for example, may need applied algebra rather than college algebra. Similarly, English classes might provide such a student with invaluable training in technical writing; study of Sophocles might not be necessary.

In many schools, the academic classes designed for vocational students—often informally prefixed "shop"—are terminal programs: They offer limited information and lead nowhere.

Graduates of such programs who later attempt to further their education face a struggle. The limited scope of their vocational courses does not adequately prepare them for community college or associate-degree programs, let alone baccalaureate-degree programs.

A smarter and harder-working labor force will be essential as the nation strives to regain its industrial competitiveness. Today's vocational-education students will make up the backbone of that force.

In Taiwan, 70 percent of all students are enrolled in vocational-education programs. There are seven vocational-education high schools for each academic high school. The reverse ratio would better describe the situation in the United States, where often one vocational school must serve many districts.

Yet a directory of occupations released by the U.S. Labor Department indicates that only 20 percent of the jobs listed require a college degree. The other 80 percent call for the types of skills usually taught in vocational-education programs.

While some familiar jobs of the past—such as that of machine operator—are disappearing, new ones are taking their place. Forecasts of the future job market identify, for instance, a growing need for office-machine service technicians and data-processing-machine mechanics. In the building trades, more sophisticated systems, such as climate-controlled environments, will require service from workers familiar with computerized technology.

> Schools are obliged to provide a sound academic education for all of their students, and the calls for excellence have brought about some positive changes. But we must remember that American schools serve a wide range of students and that the future needs of the non-college-bound deserve equal attention. In the interest not only of equity but also of economic growth, we must maintain effective vocational-education programs.
>
> (Reprinted with permission from Education Week, Vol. 7, No. 27, March 30, 1988. Reprinted by permission of the author.)

year of formal education, after all, is a year of formal education—according to the current state of the art in human capital research. However, it may well be that the degrees and credentials themselves are the object of increasing years of formal instruction, not the content of the education.

Other economists argue that a college diploma is more a signal of individual ability than an indicator of achievement directly related to productive employment. A student who has gone through college and graduated shows that he or she has the ability to be more extensively trained after college. rather than that he or she has learned the particulars of any given occupation. Under this "screening" interpretation, extra years of formal education required by employers are primarily placed before young people as hurdles to be mastered before they are deemed eligible for employment.[1] Therefore, students are encouraged and frequently aided by their parents to get into a good school and get good grades, regardless of whether they can actually perform some occupationally relevant skill upon graduation. Importantly, variations of this screening model have also been used to describe aspects of the movement of Japanese students from secondary schools through college and into their world of work.[2]

Many critics of the human resource development function of higher education contend that most prestigious colleges and universities still remain essentially antivocational. Furthermore, the supposed success of graduates from such institutions stems not primarily from any occupationally relevant skills developed in colleges and universities, but rather from the personal contacts made during four years of fun and games on campus. The sociologist Randall Collins, for example, argues that the rise in importance of the university in American life from the 1950s through the 1970s *followed* rather than preceded the rapid technological advances and economic development of the United States during this period:

> College attendance had become an interlude of fun in the lives of upper-class and upper-middle-class young Americans, and the rise of enrollments must be partly attributed to the rising standard of living. But the rituals of undergraduate life had another important aspect: they were direct expressions of the informal side of stratification, sociability. Through participation in the parties and pranks of college life, young

Americans formed and consolidated friendships. . . . The collegiate culture took the function of bringing together the children of the upper middle class, forming them into groups of friends bound together by sentiments of college activities and eventually intermarrying.[3]

Others agree that credentials are used to screen potential workers in the United States, yet emphasize even more than Collins that secondary school completion, college enrollment, and "college persistence" are as much predicted by race and social class as they are by ability. In other words, the screening of children based on differences other than talent occurs throughout the educational process for all children, not just for the smaller percentage of college graduates seeking employment at age 22 or 23.[4] Credentialism under this interpretation is not only an inefficient way to produce skilled labor for the economy, but also counterproductive to interests of equality of opportunity (see Box 9.2).

ARE AMERICAN WORKERS EDUCATIONALLY OVERQUALIFIED?

If human capital interpretations of the relevance of advanced years of education are weakened by credentialist arguments, they are even further challenged by a number of studies in the 1970s and 1980s regarding the "overeducation" of many high school and college graduates. Notwithstanding the claim that ever-increasing years of formal schooling lead to greater worker productivity (the human capital argument), and counter to contemporary school reform advocates that declare that Americans today lack many of the occupational skills necessary for productive employment, several studies of highly educated Americans have suggested quite the reverse.

In a famous study of worker productivity among lower-skilled white-collar and semiprofessional workers, Ivar Berg found that those with minimum educational qualifications in a variety of occupations performed better than those with more advanced coursework in their chosen fields.[5] In this research, neither workers nor their supervisors were satisfied with occupational conditions after extra job-related schooling, even though the workers typically obtained such training at the request of employers. After the employee completed additional credential requirements, immediate supervisors typically complained about the inefficiency of their better trained employees, and such employees complained they were overqualified for the work they previously felt comfortable with.

Others have made similiar observations during the past decade with regard to current relationships between college education and the structure of occupational opportunities in America. According to studies by Val

BOX 9.2   **Where Will Future Trade and Technical Workers Come From If They Are All Pushed toward College?**

Study Cites Pressures on Vocational Education

By Reagan Walker

The combined impact of a declining student population and education reforms that have raised academic requirements may produce an enrollment war between vocational schools and comprehensive high schools, preliminary data from the National Assessment of Vocational Education suggest.

Findings from the first of three interim reports to be issued as part of the federally mandated study indicate that enrollment in vocational programs is declining faster than the school-age population.

And one byproduct of that decline has been strained relations between vocational officials and high-school counselors and administrators, says the report.

In New York State, for example, enrollments in vocational programs fell by 6.7 percent between 1982 and 1986, while overall secondary-school enrollments decreased by 5.1 percent. Similar declines have been documented in California and elsewhere, according to the report.

The competition for students such declines have fostered, it says, has become so intense in some locales that school administrators there consider public relations a large part of their job. Maintaining enrollment, they told researchers, is one of their major functions.

Vocational administrators in New York and other sites visited by the NAVE research team complained that officials at comprehensive high schools urge their counselors and teachers to discourage students from attending an area facility.

Some districts may limit the overall number of students they will support at a vocational school, the officials said, and others will often direct the most "costly" students, such as the handicapped, to the area facility.

In particular, the vocational administrators reported, they are finding it increasingly difficult to gain access to middle-school students, an age group they would like to make more aware of high-school vocational programs. Guidance counselors, they said, contribute to that difficulty.

The study suggests that recent academic reforms have exacerbated the problems brought about by declining overall enrollments.

It cites such specific reforms as increases in the number of units in core or academic courses required for graduation and the introduction of advanced diplomas or special certificates for additional academic coursework.

These new requirements place growing—and often competing—demands on students' time, the report says, and contribute to enrollment declines not only in area vocational schools, but also in vocational programs offered at comprehensive high schools.

(Reprinted with permission from Education Week, *Vol. 7, No. 22, February 24, 1988.)*

Burris and Russell Rumberger, for example, many college graduates apparently cannot find work even remotely reflective of their training.[6] Contrary to current claims, then, that America is internationally unproductive because its citizens lack a pool of talents, such economists argue that at the upper end of the educational spectrum (at least) we have too many "overeducated" Americans who either cannot be absorbed into the economy, or who now must take jobs that were formerly held by high school students (an argument advanced by Thomas Green; see Chapter 8).

MIGHT OTHER TYPES OF INSTITUTIONS BETTER TRAIN FUTURE AMERICAN WORKERS?

Each of the preceding perspectives and research findings, of course, does damage to conventional human capital arguments. Some economists argue that the pursuit of educational degrees and credentials by high school and college students is an end only partly justifiable with regard to the skills being learned in school. Others tend to agree with mainstream social scientists that employers may be using the school primarily to locate future workers with occupationally appropriate abilities, attitudes, and values that would allow them to be specifically trained *after* their general schooling.

Furthermore, even specific vocational and occupational training programs in secondary schools have proven inefficient in the formation of human capital, according to some sociologists. That is, coursework specifically undertaken for employment during high school and college is frequently unappreciated both by educators and many employers. For example, vocational schools are the only secondary school setting specifically targeted to making students employable upon graduation. Yet their graduates have been no more successful at obtaining adequate jobs during the past several decades than those who learned similiar trades in the armed forces or in apprenticeship programs. As Randall Collins notes:

> Vocational education in the schools for manual positions is virtually irrelevant to job fate. . . . A major reason for the failure of vocational schooling is probably that vocational high schools are known as places where youthful troublemakers are sent to remove them from the regular schools. The warfare between teachers and students at a regular high school is considered mild compared with the real gang-type violence (often with ethnic or racial overtones) that is reputed to occur at "Tech." Even if a vocational student happens to learn some usable skills, his or her attendance at a vocational school is likely to be taken by the discerning employer as a sign of bad character.[7]

Another interesting criticism of conventional "education for economic development" purposes (specifically in rural America) has been put forth by

Jonathan Sher. He tends to agree that the secondary school could be used for economic development, but finds it odd that directly teaching high school students entrepreneurial skills for starting up their own businesses is never part of the secondary school curriculum. Instead, high schools ought to do so and should even allow and encourage students to use the high school and its services for start-up operations. Then secondary education could really aid in the process of *local* economic development, rather than in encouraging students to leave their home communities in order to swell the ranks of college campuses and the army of job-seekers scouting for employment opportunities in larger cities.[8]

The bottom line, then, for many sociologists and labor economists (whose more critical works have conveniently escaped the notice of many school reformers) is that human capital formation may take place in a variety of social and occupational settings, including the school. How to disentangle the effects of instruction on occupational placement or on larger economic development factors, however, is no simple matter. Certainly the notion that years of schooling completed "explains" this phenomenon is theoretically disputed among them. Meanwhile, a variety of sociologists specifically interested in the process of economic development have argued that years of public schooling completed in the United States is tightly bound up with a number of economically *related* factors (e.g., social status), but that such factors seem *independent* of economic productivity concerns.

ALTERNATIVE ROUTES TO EDUCATION FOR HUMAN CAPITAL FORMATION

Contrary to the conventional wisdom, then, while current calls for school reform frequently couch their rhetoric in economic terms, many economists want no part of the credit. In addition to the neoclassical argument that returning public schools to the private sector might "improve" consumer control of schooling, there is a second, yet related neoclassical argument against transforming public schools as they now exist into resource centers for enhancing economic productivity. In essence, this argument suggests that there are multiple ways to achieve particular economic ends. For example, rather than attempting to completely redirect existing educational institutions into skill development centers for the private sector, could not a number of alternative institutional settings be developed? Why not divert some public taxes away from secondary schools and colleges to greatly expand community college systems, work study programs, vocational/technical centers, and business-controlled training sites? (See Boxes 9.3 and 9.4.) Assuming that our government leaders were truly interested in using public monies for the formation of human capital, and given the demonstrated "inefficiencies" schools have shown in so doing, why not save lots of time and trouble by breaking up this "monopoly"?

BOX 9.3 **Alternative Routes for Upgrading Worker Skills?**

Panel Calls for Ties between Schools, Community Colleges

By Robert Rothman

WASHINGTON—Community colleges should strengthen their links with schools to help broaden educational and job-training opportunities for disadvantaged youths, a national commission concludes in a new report.

Such efforts, it says, should include beginning student recruitment as early as junior high school and making some programs available to 11th and 12th graders.

The two-year institutions' "explosive" growth over the past 40 years, said Ernest L. Boyer, the panel's chairman, represents "the greatest success story in postwar American higher education."

"Community colleges have been the colleges of choice for minority students, disproportionately to their percentage of the total population," Mr. Boyer, president of the Carnegie Foundation for the Advancement of Teaching, said at a press conference here last week. "That, we celebrate."

However, he added, such institutions must do more to help minority youths complete school and obtain postsecondary training.

In particular, the report recommends, two-year colleges should develop new four-year programs in cooperation with high schools and four-year colleges, and strengthen their core academic curricula.

Most of the proposals would require institutions to "reshift priorities," rather than spend a great deal of money, according to Dale Parnell, president of the American Association of Community and Junior Colleges, which sponsored the report. He said the panel would remain in existence for another two or three years to monitor the implementation of its recommendations.

"Undervalued" Sector

The commission's report, "Building Communities," assesses the future of a sector of education that has been "undervalued and unrecognized" by school and college reformers, according to Mr. Boyer.

Despite that lack of attention, the report notes, community colleges have become "the largest single sector of higher education in the United States."

Enrollment at community colleges grew by 240 percent between 1965 and 1975, it says, and now represents some 43 percent of the nation's undergraduates and 51 percent of first-time freshmen.

The country's 1,224 two-year colleges will become increasingly critical to the economy in the next decade, according to Mr. Parnell, because the overwhelming majority of new jobs will require some postsecondary training.

"The associate degree will take on new importance in that environment," he said. "It provides a quality assurance to employers that their employees can read, write, and compute."

But in order to meet that challenge, the report says, community colleges must "define, with greater clarity and sophistication, their distinctive mission."

"Early Identification"

In particular, it states, community colleges must enroll more minority students and ensure that they complete their courses of study.

"This, then, is the central mandate," it says. "The community college must continue to offer all students an open door, and reaffirm to minority students the promise of empowerment through education."

To that end, the report recommends that each college create an "early identification program" with local schools, focusing on junior-high-school students. These programs would provide counseling and language instruction to ensure that students have the proper academic preparation for postsecondary instruction, the report says.

Once students are enrolled, it adds, the colleges should ensure that they remain until they receive degrees. It urges community colleges to reduce their dropout rates by 50 percent over the next decade.

General Education

Community colleges must also restructure their instructional programs to include a core general-education curriculum for all students, the report concludes.

Currently, about two-thirds of community-college students are enrolled in career and technical studies, and few of these receive instruction in academic subjects, it notes.

"I worry that we prepare people for short-term job entry, who perhaps lack the language skills that make them able to be more flexible in the job market," said Mr. Boyer.

To ensure that all students receive both types of preparation, the report urges schools and community colleges to join together in arrangements that allow students to begin technical training in the last two years of high school and complete their studies in two years of college.

In addition, it proposes, four-year colleges should encourage "inverted degree" programs that enable students to follow a two-year specialized program in a community college, followed by two years of general-education studies in a four-year institution.

The report also recommends that:

Community colleges become models for effective teaching. Such institutions, it says, "should define the role of the faculty member as classroom researcher —focusing evaluation on instruction and making a clear connection between what the teacher teaches and how students learn."

Arrangements facilitating students' transfer from two-year to four-year colleges be strengthened.

"While not every two-year student should move on to complete the baccalaureate degree," Mr. Boyer said, "the need to keep this option open, especially for black and Hispanic students, is essential."

Copies of the report, "Building Communities: A Vision for a New Century," can be ordered, at $15 per copy, by calling, toll free, (800) 336-4776, or in Virginia, (703) 823-6966. They can also be purchased from the American Association of Community and Junior Colleges, Publications Department, 80 South Early St., Alexandria, Va. 22304.

(Reprinted with permission from Education Week, *Vol. 7, No. 31, April 27, 1988.)*

BOX 9.4   Can Employment Opportunities Help Keep Students from Dropping Out of School?

Employment Strategies for Dropout Prevention

By Victor Herbert

For many of us, the process of preparing for and finding a job is almost automatic. We grow up assuming that we will work someday. And we are told about the steps required to get there: summer jobs, internships, college.

Our daily dealings with parents, friends, and relatives do much to reinforce these assumptions: Conversations may concern the day's accomplishments at work, complaints about a boss, the amount of a paycheck, or the need to find a better job. Even the sound of an alarm clock, or a morning radio show, announces that something important—the work day—has begun.

Yet many of the students at risk for dropping out of school—such as those participating in New York City's Dropout Prevention Program—have not had these kinds of experiences. Growing up in an environment largely composed of non-workers, they conceive of work in an abstract way. Such students may say that they want to be doctors, lawyers, or sports stars, but they have no idea about how to fulfill those dreams.

This should not surprise us; how could it be otherwise? Surrounded by the devastating effects of poverty and unemployment, these youngsters have few role models to follow in the pursuit of a career or a vocation. Moreover, they feel frustrated, angry, and hopeless as they watch their friends and relatives struggle to free themselves from the vicious cycles of poverty.

Statistics reveal only a small part of the story:

About two-thirds of the students in New York City's 10 D.P.P. high schools come from single-parent homes, in many of which the struggle to find work and to survive economically is constant.

Anywhere from 50 to 75 percent of the students in some D.P.P. high schools live in households where the annual income falls below the poverty line.

In 1987, the average unemployment rate for blacks of all ages in New York City was 9.2 percent—nearly twice the 4.7 percent rate for whites. The unemployment rate for Hispanics during the same period was 8.8 percent.

One consequence of the reality that these figures suggest is that inner-city teen-agers lack a stable frame of reference for the pursuit of employment. Anticipating a bleak future, they feel that finding a rewarding job is virtually impossible. For the Dropout Prevention Program, this situation presents an enormous challenge: How should this milieu be addressed—and undone—to prepare students for the challenges of an increasingly sophisticated, technologically-based economy?

Two-and-a-half years ago, Mayor Edward Koch established our program—giving us $10 million for 10 high schools—to confront these kinds of issues. Of the various dropout-prevention strategies with which the program has experimented, one of the most important has been the effort to link earning with learning through the development of comprehensive part-time and full-time employment programs for at-risk students. We have learned several lessons thus far.

As a fundamental principle, employment opportunities must be part of any dropout-prevention effort. Working can nourish self-esteem and can give youngsters a feeling of belonging in spite of the hardships confronted at home and in their neighborhoods. Because it relates education to long-term economic independence, a job also motivates students to atttend school and obtain a diploma. Finally, professional experiences can teach students about such values as responsibility to others, punctuality, and discipline.

Employment, then, can be an effective anti-dropout strategy, particularly when it is used as an incentive for disadvantaged youths to stay in school. Through the efforts of school personnel and community-based organizations in the D.P.P. high schools, hundreds of part-time jobs—within the schools, in local businesses, or in the public sector—have been found for teen-agers who are at risk of dropping out.

The opportunity to win a part-time job in return for good attendance and achievement can be enormously stabilizing to youngsters who are living in turmoil. While this approach departs from the practice of many other employment programs, which reward youngsters who are already succeeding in school, we have found that the offer of a job induces many potential dropouts to remain in school.

(*Reprinted with permission from* Education Week, *Vol. 7, No. 18, January 27, 1988. Reprinted by permission of the author.*)

In actuality, several important arguments of just this type have been forwarded during the past decade, frequently by social scientists. Margaret Mead, for example, suggested educational changes in the 1960s that could just as easily be proposed today.[9] She claimed that during the nineteenth and early twentieth centuries, public education through high school may have been appropriate. The jobs most Americans entered during this period were relatively stable, and it made good sense for children to spend quite a bit of time preparing for occupations they would continue in until retirement. However, she argued, occupations in modern times change very rapidly, as do the competencies necessary for their successful completion. Furthermore, she suggests, the last place to train future citizens of this planet is in outmoded institutions like our public schools, whose instructors are wedded to forms of knowledge and authority from previous generations.

Instead of expecting and forcing children to prepare for an indefinite future *before* they leave school, Mead claims that a reasonable and efficient society should make it possible for young adults to leave school earlier, yet at the same time institute policies whereby adults can continually return for additional educational training when they deem it necessary. Mead suggests that keeping students in school longer and longer is economically counterproductive, as much of what they learn in public schools is out of date even as they enter adulthood. Furthermore, extending school attendance requirements into the late teens and early twenties is socially counterproductive. Here, she argues, the desire to emulate adulthood within the artificial confines of America's high schools and colleges brings about an adolescent subculture frequently at odds with the larger social needs of America.

One chronicler of the occupational implications of post-industrial society appears somewhat in agreement with previously discussed school reform perspectives. He too argues that we now reside in an explosive information-based society and are dependent on research and development frequently undertaken in advanced university centers of technology. Yet, his (limited) pronouncement on what public schooling is necessary for most Americans in the future sounds somewhat more like Margaret Mead's than it does like those made by the National Committee on Excellence in Education. According to David Birch:

> The rate at which people change careers (not jobs) is now 10 percent per year, not per decade as once it was. Under these circumstances, we cannot possibly create a competitive labor force by simply improving the relevance and quality of what schools teach, although even this would be difficult to accomplish. . . . [This] means that education must be constant, on the job, with much of it acquired through what passes for journalism.[10]

From Birch's perspective, then, a sound basic education, good grounding in general knowledge, and learning how to learn are all required for our post-industrial society. And years of formal education in colleges and universities would appear to be much less useful in the future than adequate nonformal and informal educational opportunities throughout the course of one's (multiple) careers.

On the other hand, James Coleman and his associates made different appeals for school reforms from those based primarily on human capital formation. In a report he and his colleagues made to then President Nixon in the early 1970s, the Coleman group argued that public education in the United States was biased *in favor of* cognitive skill instruction, not that such instruction was lacking. Furthermore, this study argued that both the economy and the students suffered from the extensive control of public schools over every aspect of their lives. For example, the Coleman panel documented very high turnover rates of high school graduates during their first year of employment. This was brought about ostensibly because students had spent too much time "academically" preparing for jobs that, once begun, turned out to be personally or socially uninteresting. The Coleman group reported that an entire host of personal and social skills necessary for individual and cultural survival was underemphasized in public education. Interestingly, their recommendations were that cognitive skills be less emphasized in the school curriculum and that children spend *fewer* hours per day in the classroom, but more hours per week learning about jobs and community life outside of the school.[11]

More recently, Coleman argued that the reforming of American schools to make them more effective ought to focus not on *human* capital, but upon *social* capital. In this analysis, Coleman reports that perceived schooling problems in America are not primarily the result of deficient curricula, but rather the result of too little parent involvement with the social and educational development of American children:

> There has been, over the past twenty-five years, an extensive erosion of social capital available to [U.S.] children and youth, both within the family and outside it. Within the family, the growth in human capital is extensive, as reflected by the increased levels of educational attainment. But the social capital, as reflected by the presence of adults in the home, and the range of exchange between parents and children about academic, social, economic, and personal matters, has declined, at the same time that the parents' human capital has grown.[12]

The implication of Coleman's analysis is that those wishing to make our public schools more "effective" would do better to develop more supportive family and community resources for children, rather than to continually seek more academic rigor only within the school building. Parenthetically, academically successful children in Japanese families seem not to lack this social capital. There, parents (particularly mothers) typically spend several hours each day in helping students with their schoolwork.[13]

COMPETING PERSPECTIVES ON WHAT IS NEEDED TO IMPROVE OUR ECONOMY

An underlying assumption of human capital theory is that understanding and changing the individual is the key to economic and social progress. Human capital arguments suggest that the individual is a rational and individual agent in search of better skills to improve his or her life chances, as well as those of society. Even modernization theory and post-industrial perspectives typically focus on the impact of modern institutions on the individual, or talk of the individual characteristics necessary to participate in social life. Yet, at least since the writings of Robert Owen and Karl Marx, there have been arguments that it is the human community that ought to be the first concern of those interested in understanding and furthering the process of economic and social change.

Human capitalists, business leaders, and many policy makers for example, conceive of society as the location where individuals develop and market their occupational skills. Our current problem, we are told, is that countries like Japan are more productive than we are because their workers have better skills. Yet, a number of mainstream economists have recently questioned assumptions that individual skill levels are the essential difference between Japanese productivity and our own. Rather, economists like Lester Thurow, Henry Levin, and Russell Rumberger have begun to argue that production incentive systems and the social organization of the workplace are primarily responsible for productivity differences between the United States and our international competition.

While Lester Thurow seems in general rather skeptical of key aspects of human capital theory, he tends to agree with many of the critics of contemporary education and calls for more achievement orientation within American schools. Yet, he argues, combating economic decline in the United States is only partly related to worker skill deficiencies. Rather, our unfavorable international trade situation is just as clearly related to a lack of committed leadership in the private sector of the economy. For example, rather than investing in physical capital related to long-term productivity (such as is done in Japan), according to Thurow the dominant management style in America currently is directed at short-term goals. In nations where employees and managers expect and are expected to have long-term career patterns within a particular company, long-term decision making and investments are the norm. In the United States, however, late twentieth-century management incentive programs are typically based on quarterly earnings, and both managers and workers more typically move from company to company as product lines rise and fall. Therefore, short-term profitability schemes (like buying another company) are attractive routes to immediate success, but little related to long-term excellence in design and manufacture. Making our economy internationally competitive, therefore, entails a national commitment to product excellence as well as educational excellence.

In a somewhat different appeal, Thurow also counters the claim that reforming elementary and secondary education alone would greatly improve skilled "manpower" requirements for our economy. This economist believes that federal investments in education for the non-college-bound need to dramatically increase in the coming years (an appeal rarely heard from school reform panels full of higher education representatives). Interestingly, his analysis and argument moderately resembles the positions of Margaret Mead and Russell Rumberger:

> During recessions America's failure to train enough skilled non-college workers is hidden, but shortages become apparent whenever unemployment falls. What do employers complain about in tight labor markets? Certainly not an inability to hire unskilled workers or college-educated labor. Complaints almost always focus on shortages of skilled blue-collar workers—machinists, tool and die makers, etc. . . . . subsid[ies] should

. . . be given to the non-college bound in the form of a skill voucher that they could gradually cash over their working lifetime at any approved employer training program.[14]

In addition to analyzing what they claim are poor incentive models for current economic competitiveness in American industry, Thurow, Levin, and Rumberger also contend that management styles used in the United States are inefficient for economic productivity. Thurow argues that removing job execution from management has proven to be inefficient (see the discussion in Chapter 4). In more productive economies (like Japan's), workers and managers operate in a teamlike manner, and worker input and insight into production processes are expected rather than discouraged.

Levin and Rumberger make similar observations with respect to how the workplace ought to be organized, based on their observations that many American workers are overqualified, rather than underqualified for their jobs. Levin, for example, suggests that economic productivity of the United States could be significantly enhanced were we to better utilize the individual skills many American workers *already* possess, rather than continue to believe that the lack of such skills is what is responsible for our current economic situation. According to Levin:

> Traditional organization of work in hierarchical firms separates the planning, execution, and evaluation of work. Planning is set out by high level managers and technical personnel who design the production process. Execution is done by the majority of workers who follow the job tasks set out by the planners. Evaluation is done by supervisors who try to assure that workers are meeting the work and product standards set out by the planning process. This approach not only exacts a heavy price among most workers who are given relatively unchallenging and repetitive jobs, but it also deprives the firm of insights that workers might contribute to the planning and evaluation phases that might improve productivity.[15]

"RADICAL" CRITIQUES OF HUMAN CAPITAL THEORY

Many arguments suggest either that lack of worker skills is not the main problem with our economy, or that applying human capital theory uncritically via our public school system would be inadequate for dramatically improving American economic productivity. In either case, more systematic study of workplace demands and training needs has typically been called for by a variety of economists, not just a unilateral upgrading of academic skills for all high school and college students. A number of economists have placed just as much if not more blame upon industry leaders and the federal government for the decline in American productivity during the past decade.

**BOX 9.5   How Easily Could Workplace Democracy
Be Put Into Effect in the U.S.?**

Profits Dip, But Executive Salaries? Never!

By Rick Gladstone (Associated Press)

NEW YORK—Lee A. Iacocca made enough money last year to buy a fleet of more than 1,500 Chrysler Le Barons, while his company lost market share to rival automakers and its profits fell 7 percent.

Put another way, a worker toiling at minimum wage for 40 hours a week since the birth of Christ probably wouldn't have earned as much as the $38.43 million Iacocca collected in the last two years from salary, bonuses and exercised stock options, AFL-CIO economists have calculated.

The example reflects what labor activists and some compensation consultants call an irrational and unfair system for awarding America's corporate executives.

Defenders of the system say it's dictated by the law of supply and demand, as well as the enormous stress chief executives endure in an increasingly competitive world.

Critics contend the system allows both the best and worst talent to lock in millions of dollars in compensation for years into the future. They say it's also a system that doesn't necessarily reward risk or penalize failure.

For example, oil giant Texaco Inc., reeling from bankruptcy proceedings and a record $4.4 billion loss last year that caused it to suspend three dividend payments, awarded a 14 percent pay raise to James W. Kinnear, who replaced John McKinley as chief executive at the end of 1986. That raised Kinnear's salary to nearly $723,000.

According to an analysis by Towers Perrin Forster & Crosby, a leading management consulting firm, the median total cash compensation—salary plus annual bonus—for chief executives in the nation's largest industrial companies passed the $1 million mark for the first time last year.

Just among the 30 companies that comprise the Dow Jones industrial average, which tumbled 22.6 percent in value Black Monday, Oct. 19, chief executive pay in 1987 doubled in some cases, excluding long-term compensation.

For example, Navistar International's James C. Cotting made $640,000, up 113 percent; Merck & Co.'s P. Roy Vagelos made $1.37 million, up 42 percent; USX Corp.'s David Roderick made $1.36 million, up 85 percent.

When long-term compensation such as stock options and restricted stock grants are factored in, the figures can multiply rapidly and aren't necessarily related to a company's size or profitability.

A stock option is a right to purchase stock at a set price in the future. Restricted stock is owned but cannot be sold for a period of time, usually three to five years. Both are heavily used in management pay packages in order to retain valued executives.

An annual survey done by Business Week found the highest-paid executive in the land last year was Jim P. Manzi, chairman of Lotus Development Corp., who made $26.3 million, mostly from gains realized on stock options.

Ford Motor Co.'s chairman and chief executive Donald Peterson made $3.37 million. His chief operating officer Harold Poling made $10.55 million, largely because he exercised stock options and Peterson didn't.

In the case of Iacocca, No. 2 on the Business Week list, much of his $17.9 million of compensation last year also came from exercising stock options. They were granted under a 1983 agreement designed to keep him at the helm of the automaker that he helped save from bankruptcy earlier this decade.

Defenders of Iacocca's compensation argue that he took a substantial risk in turning the company around and the stock would be worthless today if it hadn't been for his talented leadership.

In response to questions about his $20.54 million pay in 1986, Iacocca himself said: "That's the American way. If little kids don't aspire to make money like I did, what the hell good is this country?"

Unionists call Iacocca's pay exorbitant and a slap in the face at the Chrysler workers, especially in a year when the automaker's profits fell and management exhorted labor to cut waste.

"We find the Iacocca thing excessive," said John Zalusky, an AFL-CIO economist who specializes in collective bargaining. "The workers there made a greater contribution and sacrifice than he did."

How Iacocca and other top U.S. bosses obtain lucrative pay packages often involves a complicated process that begins in the executive boardroom, where a compensation committee of outside directors evaluates management performance.

The directors often are busy executives themselves and must rely on the recommendations of an independent compensation consultant, who in some cases has been hired by the boss himself.

"The directors can be misled," said Jude Rich, president of Sibson & Co., a large compensation consultant firm based in Princeton, N.J. "Unfortunately, there's more of that than there should be."

Another reason the boss's pay keeps rising is that boards are afraid of losing top executives, Rich said. It's quite rare that a board will tell management to take a compensation cut.

"That's a weighty thing. What if you're wrong?" Rich said. "So 15 of your top guys walk and go to someone else. Then we have a debacle on our hands. The leverage you get from keeping top executives happy is very high, so boards err on the side of being careful."

(Reprinted from the Lexington Herald Leader, *May 1, 1988, with the permission of the Associated Press.)*

Rebuilding the American economy, these economists suggest, calls for corporate and business reforms more so than it does for school reforms (see Box 9.5). Such reforms include teamwork, more cooperation between managers and workers, and group incentive strategies; otherwise, workers become disaffected and uncommitted to company objectives and overall productivity. Low-productivity problems are as much or more a function of poor management and leadership style as they are attributable to workers' lack of skills. Importantly, investments in human capital may not pay off in many jobs because the capital is underutilized; the key to future economic success is to better utilize much of what is already available.

While such interpretations continue to be researched and debated, a number of economists from more critical traditions question whether currently called for economic reforms are possible within our current social and political system. Even Thurow suggests that the job restructuring he thinks necessary demands a new political agenda, not just an economic one. Meanwhile, those further to the left continue to argue that our economic system actually serves more the needs of those in control of the economy rather than the bulk of our citizens. Furthermore, they typically view the current school reform agenda as yet another effort to convince those who suffer from our economic problems that they themselves are the cause of them.

Paradoxically, while many observers of the relationship between American business and our public schools contend (as I do) that the needs of business have always been central to its functioning, many also contend that the school has historically served as a convenient scapegoat when economic problems not of its own making have emerged. Joel Spring, for example, contends that current business concerns over the supposed lack of employable youth are primarily the result of changes in demographic characteristics of American society during the past three decades. When the "baby boomers" first entered the labor market in the 1960s and 1970s, employers made free use of an oversupply of labor, and therefore failed to invest in the new technologies they would need in the future. According to Spring, employers cared little about educational "excellence" in this country when they could pick and choose from among too many applicants for every position. Now, however, with fewer applicants to pick from, they have again become very interested in what education can do for them, especially given the fact that they must now catch up technologically with the rest of the world. According to Spring:

> If the schools continue to be geared to meet the changing needs of U.S. business, we can expect still another change in educational policy in the next decade to meet those changing desires. Thus the public school system becomes a captive of the profit motive of U.S. industry. And, let me emphasize again, this relationship guarantees neither an improved economy nor a higher standard of living for individuals. Indeed, such a close connection between education and industry might lead to *lower* wages, as different segments of the labor market are flooded by workers channeled there by the public school system. In effect, American business would be using the public school system to exploit the American worker.[16]

DUAL LABOR MARKETS AND THE SYSTEMATIC UNDERUTILIZATION OF HUMAN CAPITAL

As Spring suggests, many radical economists theoretically dispute what have now become conventional economics of education approaches to "improving the quality of our workforce." In their judgment, human capital theory is deficient because it argues that competencies of workers are primary determinants of the types of jobs available and carried out. Instead, such economists believe, the jobs many Americans have are determined by the types of jobs the private sector creates. Barry Bluestone, for example, criticized the human capital movement of the 1960s and 1970s, which suggested that increasing educational opportunities and training programs would lead to more and better jobs, particularly for those at the bottom of the economic distribution. Rather, he argued that training workers for nonexistent careers was a cruel hoax played upon those who could least afford it:

> For many of the low-paid, low wages are not due to lack of education or human capital. Low wages are mainly the result of entrapment in low-wage, nondurable, manufacturing firms, retail-trade establishments, service industries, and, to some extent, wholesale trade. Being black, brown or female is often sufficient to narrow occupational choice to a low-wage clerical, operator, laborer, or service position in one of these industries. . . . Given the opportunity to escape to the high-wage sector, many low-wage workers would perform admirably. Without years of extra education, without massive doses of institutional and on-the-job training, without learning a new "industrial discipline," many low-wage workers could fit into a unionized, profitable, capital-intensive industry and begin to earn a living wage.[17]

As such an analysis suggests, many critical economists suggest that focusing on the supply of human skills to explain economic inequality and lack of productivity is a theoretical mistake. In their view, our economy is built on a segmented labor force, where some jobs are defined as information based and/or management oriented, while others are created and defined as low-skilled, low-status, and low-income. Furthermore, acquisition of productive skills has less to do with how one obtains a position within the segmented labor market, than with one's ethnicity, gender, values, appearance, and other personal features (see Table 9.1). If all workers were actually paid in accordance with their stock of human skills, the costs of business would be too high for most employers. As C. O'Donnell explains:

> Whilst neoclassical theory emphasises equilibrium theory and even development within the labour market, dual labour market theory sees uneven economic development as the more common situation. Neoclassical theorists are prone to discuss the characteristics of workers as the major determinants of the labour market; dual labour market theorists emphasise demand, rather than supply, factors.[18]

Dual labor theorists, typically coming from a Marxist perspective, doubt that enhancing the human capital of workers will have positive impact on their ability to better their occupational futures now, or that optimistic

TABLE 9.1. MEDIAN WEEKLY EARNINGS OF FULL-TIME WAGE AND SALARY WORKERS, BY RACE AND SEX, ANNUAL AVERAGES, 1981

Years of School Completed	All Races			White			Black			Hispanic		
	Both sexes	Men	Women	Both sexes	Men	Women	Both sexes	Men	Women	Both sexes	Men	Women
Total, 25 years and over	316	378	237	325	389	239	251	290	220	246	282	201
Less than 4 years of high school	242	290	180	249	301	182	211	241	172	210	232	167
8 years of school or less	227	259	169	232	268	171	203	225	160	199	221	158
1 to 3 years of high school	256	314	187	268	326	190	217	257	177	235	266	185
4 years of high school or more	333	402	249	341	409	251	273	317	237	293	349	234
4 years of high school	291	363	222	298	372	224	243	294	209	264	319	211
1 to 3 years of college	334	398	259	342	405	261	283	325	246	316	370	258
4 years of college or more	417	482	325	422	490	326	350	396	326	371	414	308
4 years of college	393	459	299	402	471	301	321	354	296	340	384	285
5 years of college or more	443	507	362	445	510	359	416	449	384	421	446	(¹)

[1] Median not shown where base is less than 50,000.

(Source: Earl F. Mellor and George D. Stamas, "Usual Weekly Earnings: Another Look at Intergroup Differences and Basic Trends" [Monthly Labor Review, April 1987, p. 16.])

schemes to "democraticize the workplace" in the future can be easily effected in the United States. This is because, as they would argue, the *technical* division of labor has become centrally linked to the *social* relations of production in American capitalism. As the division of labor has proceeded and continues to proceed in the workplace, the duties of managers and workers continue to be seen as separate undertakings. Furthermore, low-status and low-skill occupations continue to be created within our economy, and these jobs continue to be "reserved" for those already at the bottom of the economic order.

HOW SCHOOLS "PREPARE" STUDENTS
FOR THE DUAL LABOR MARKET

Radical economists like Samuel Bowles and Herbert Gintis interpret the economic possibilities of schooling quite differently from the human capital economists. Human capital theory posits that decisions to invest in the future are rationally accomplished by individuals who weigh their "opportunity costs" based on anticipated economic returns to their educational investment. At the same time, the dominant conviction of many Americans (both in the workplace and in the school) has been that differences in occupational and educational attainment are primarily the result of talent differences among individuals. Therefore, schools have historically sought to "weed out" students thought to possess less talent. In the school, of course, such logic underlies curved grading scales and the fascination school personnel have with norm-referenced tests.

The net effect of being "informed" by teachers and administrators (through grades and counseling sessions) that one is below average in academic ability and performance is that students with diminishing belief in their native abilities may make different sorts of "rational" choices with regard to educational "opportunity costs." Put more simply, if student "A" has been convinced that his or her ability is not as great as that of student "B," he or she may be less willing to defer entering into the labor market until later. Yet, what evidence do we currently have that differences in academic talent explain most of the differences in occupational attainment and/or economic productivity? According to Bowles and Gintis, we have very little proof. Rather, better predictors of adult economic success might be family background and years of education completed. Therefore, the ideology (or unproven belief) that individual intellectual differences predict worker productivity differences provides a convenient mechanism for assignment to better or lower paying jobs and careers.[19]

Furthermore, a number of "interpretive" social theorists now suggest that "objective" indicators of student ability and talent are not the only criteria used by teachers or by students in evaluating their educational present or future. Rather, the classroom is a setting for continual interpretation, negotiation, compliance, or resistance between and among students and teachers. Yet, since students and teachers frequently come from different social and/or ethnic origins, student performance and behaviors are typically attributed to individual cognitive and/or motivational differences, rather than to those which are the result of differences in the "lived culture" of students outside the school.

Under this interpretation, the classroom and the school become places where participants, possessing different types and amounts of "cultural capital," must negotiate face to face with others from potentially different backgrounds. Unfortunately, if those in power (typically teachers) define minority or low-income student behavior as cognitively or socally "deviant," such students may evaluate the school's potential for serving their needs negatively. Thus minority or low-income students may be rejected by the school as they simultaneously begin to reject the school's potential as a site for "investing" in their "human capital."

For example, the concept of academic work or effect is central to the functioning of today's public schools. Yet, the meaning and importance of school work may be disputed and rejected by students coming from or participating in non-middle-class environments (or operating in low-status jobs within the dual labor market) outside of the school. The British sociologist Peter Woods suggests that classroom work assigned and expected by academically oriented middle-class teachers may be responded to differently by students used to other notions about the meaning of work and intellectual effort:

> So far, I have talked about the negotiation of general rules regulating the conduct of teachers and pupils. But the kind and amount of work that pupils do, and the methods that teachers employ are also negotiated. I have said that pupils seem to view school work as a series of short-term tasks rather than as an entity with a long term rationale. But the interpretation of those tasks depends very much on the teacher and the relationships she has with her pupils, and the kinds of definitions of the situation she can persuade them to accept. In this sense, work is relationships—it is a negotiated activity. . . . For many, school work is not "real." [Students] are not paid for doing it, and to many of them, that is the crucial criterion of real work. It is often difficult for pupils to see any point in it. It has to be taken on trust for a long time, in the form of marks, grades and reports. This conception of work is reinforced by artificial stimulants which dominate the atmosphere of the school—on the one hand motivators, such as competition and inducement, appeals to vanity, pride, and one-upmanship, and on the other, penalties—reports, detentions, reporting to parents.[20]

COMPETING INTERPRETATIONS OF THE INTELLECTUAL REQUIREMENTS NECESSARY IN POST-INDUSTRIAL SOCIETY

There is a common theme in most of the conventional arguments regarding necessary skills all (or most) workers must have in a high technology society. Basically, it is argued, the future of the United States is inextricably bound up with new computer and information technologies. Furthermore, the conventional wisdom is that all Americans need to be better educated and hopefully computer-literate to deal with and take advantage of the "information age." Critics of this assessment, however, also abound, and much of their criticism also notes the ideological rather than reasoned assessment of what the actual workplace needs in American culture will be for the next several decades.

As previously discussed, however, Marxist scholars believing in dual labor market perspectives contend that the driving force behind technological development in capitalist countries has always been to reduce labor costs. In point of fact, it was argued, economic development prior to the "post-industrial" society involved the "de-skilling" of many workers, because machines and various types of automated technology took the place of skilled laborers. This reduced those involved in production either to a very few management and research and development jobs with high pay and high status, or to many unskilled and semi-skilled workers to attending to the machines.

Not surprisingly, radical economists and social scientists see that little difference in the dynamics of employment and occupational opportunity has occurred in post-industrial America, regardless of the pronouncements of contemporary school reformers. According to them, our emerging economy will continue to need a few highly literate and technologically capable workers, but also increasing numbers of service, clerical, and low-technology workers with few of the competencies claimed necessary for *all* of our citizens. For example, the fastest growing "industry" in the United States at present is the human service area (i.e., waiters, librarians, nurse's aids). In addition to the fact that such occupations may contribute little to economic productivity per se, it also seems legitimate to argue that occupational requirements for such jobs do not demand anywhere near the academic competencies typically urged by school reformers of the late twentieth century.

Martin Carnoy, for example, notes that most workers even in high-technology areas perform intellectually low-level occupational duties (like assembling pre-packaged electronic components). He further notes that those holding down lower paying and lower status jobs in high technology fields are (predictably) women and/or members of various minority groups, while white males dominate most high paying and high prestige jobs such as scientists, managers, and engineers. Citing the research of Hank Levin and Russell Rumberger, he argues:

> most new jobs will not be in high technology occupations, nor will the application of high technology to existing jobs require a vast upgrading of the skills of the American labor force. To the contrary, the expansion of the lowest skilled jobs in the American economy will vastly outstrip the growth of high technology ones. So contrary to most expectations, the vast majority of American workers will not require high levels of skill in mathematics and science or specialized training in computer skills. To the contrary, since one of the major objectives of high technology is to simplify work tasks and to reduce the skills required for jobs, most jobs in the future will not require higher level skills.[21]

SUMMARY

As we have seen in this chapter, there is an important debate within the academic community regarding the validity of human capital theory and its implications for economic development both in the past and for the future. However (yet predictably), American business and policy leaders seem only to recognize and accept one side of this debate. According to radical economists and social scientists, this is because they have typically been successful in our economic system, and believe in the merits of a "supply side" approach to human capital formation. The problem with our schools today, according to many holding such a supply side perspective, is that the skills necessary to supply continued economic expansion are not being developed adequately in American schools.

Critics of this logic note that the data supporting human capital formation through public education are meager at best and that the social and economic dynamics and consequences of education (especially that beyond basic literacy) are conveniently misunderstood by today's crusaders for school reform. Some social scientists argue that the overconcentration on economic skills in our public schools is damaging to social stability, social cohesion, and personal development.

Others note that much of education, particularly elite higher education, is vastly inefficient in the preparation of future workers. Some economists contend that employers use educational institutions as a screening device to help them select individuals who can be occupationally trained later. Furthermore, many social scientists argue that an important function of higher education has to do more with social status concerns and interests than with the acquisition of economically productive skills. While a general education *may* be important, in terms of economic productivity there is little evidence that all Americans need to go on to college, as many school reformers suggest.

Radical economists and social scientists further contend that human capital theory and the school reform reports that are linked to them do damage to the poor and working classes rather than providing them with a way out of poverty. According to them, our economy creates different types of jobs, some of which pay well and require well-trained and information-based workers, others of which are deskilled and pay comparatively little. They believe such dynamics will continue in the future. In short, they argue, our economic system is actually quite inefficient not because we have too few workers with occupationally useful skills, but rather because many workers who could contribute to the economic advance of the nation have been confined to low-status jobs where they are not allowed to be productive.

Furthermore, according to some radical scholars, the real crisis in American education today is that the schools have become the target of capitalists who have mismanaged our economy, much as they mismanaged it back in the 1920s and 1930s. Just as concerned social scientists and educators have begun to understand how to expand educational opportunities for the disadvantaged in our culture, and just when "democraticizing the workplace" seemed like a possibility in many work settings across the United States, the schools have become the target of school reformers concerned with falling economic productivity figures.

According to Stanley Aronowitz and Henry Giroux, for example, public schools are "under siege" by capitalists uninterested in democratizing the workplace and opening up the economy to full participation for disenfranchised groups. Rather, they increasingly look to public schools to turn out better skilled and more subservient workers committed to greater productivity within the confines of unequal workplaces and worker roles. To best conclude this chapter on theoretical critiques of human capital theory and contemporary school reform proposals, we end with a quote from Aronowitz and Giroux:

> Underlying [much of current] educational reform is a mode of technocratic rationality that restricts curricula and student diversity and simultaneously refuses to address seriously the issue of how to deal pedagogically with less privileged learners. In the first instance, the narrowing of curricular choices to a back-to-basics format, and the introduction of lock-step, time-on-task pedagogies operates from the pedagogically erroneous assumption that all students can learn from the same materials, pedagogies, and modes of evaluation. The notion that students come from different histories, embody different experiences, linguistic practices, cultures, and talents is ignored. Similarly, the current drive among school reformers to deny a high school diploma to students who don't pass a comprehensive graduating exam, or deny entrance to undergraduate and graduate schools to students who

don't measure up to the call for higher scores on any one of a number of tests, represents a technological solution to a highly charged political and social problem.[22]

NOTES

1. D.R. Winkler, "Screening Models and Education," in G. Psacharopoulos (ed.), *Economics and Education: Research and Studies*. Oxford: Pergamon Press, 1987, pp. 287–291.
2. U.S. Department of Education, *Japanese Education Today*. Washington, DC: U.S. Government Printing Office, 1987.
3. Randall Collins, *The Credential Society*. New York: Academic Press, 1979, pp. 124–125.
4. Paul Dimaggio, "Cultural Capital and School Success: The Impact of Status Culture Participation on the Grades of U.S. High School Students," *American Sociological Review*, 47 (April), 1982: 189–201.
5. Ivar Berg, *Education and Jobs: The Great Training Robbery*. New York: Praeger, 1970.
6. Val Burris, "The Social and Political Consequences of Overeducation," *American Sociological Review*, 48 (August); 454–467; and Russell Rumberger, *Overeducation in the U.S. Labor Market*, New York: Praeger, 1981.
7. Randall Collins, *The Credential Society*. New York: Academic Press, 1979, pp. 16–17.
8. Jonathan Sher, "Rural Development Worthy of the Name," in *New Dimensions in Rural Policy: Building Upon Our Heritage*. Joint Economic Committee Congress of the United States, Washington, DC: U.S. Government Printing Office, 1986, pp. 515–522.
9. Margaret Mead, *Culture and Commitment: A Study of the Generation Gap*. New York: Natural History Press, 1970.
10. David Birch, *Job Creation in America*. New York: The Free Press, 1987.
11. James Coleman, et al., *Youth: Transition to Adulthood*. Chicago: University of Chicago Press, 1974.
12. James Coleman, "Families and Schools," *Educational Researcher,* 16 (6), 1987; 32–38.
13. U.S. Dept. of Education, *Japanese Education Today*.
14. Lester Thurow, *The Zero Sum Solution: Building a World Class American Economy*. New York: Simon & Schuster, 1985, pp. 205–206.
15. Henry Levin, *Improving Productivity through Education and Technology*. Stanford, CA: Stanford Education Policy Institute, 1984, pp. 19–20.
16. Joel Spring, "Education and the Sony War," *Phi Delta Kappan,* (April), 1984; 534–537.
17. Barry Bluestone, "Economic Theory and the Fate of the Poor," *Social Policy,* 2 (January/February), 1972; 30–31, 46–48.
18. C. O'Donnell, "Major Theories of the Labour Market and Women's Place Within It," *Journal of Industrial Relations,* 26 (2), 1984; 147–165.

19. Samuel Bowles and Herbert Gintis, *Schooling in Capitalist America*. New York: Basic Books, 1976.
20. Peter Woods, *Sociology and the School: An Interactionist Viewpoint*. London: Routledge & Kegan Paul, 1983, p. 131.
21. Martin Carnoy, "High Technology and Education: An Economist's View," in K. Benne and S. Tozer (eds.), *Society as Educator in an Age of Transition*. Chicago: University of Chicago Press, 1987, p. 101.
22. Stanley Aronowitz and Henry Giroux, *Education Under Siege: The Conservative, Liberal and Radical Debate Over Schooling*. South Hadley, MA: Bergin and Garvey, 1985, p. 29.

FOR ADDITIONAL READING

While there is an expansive critical literature on human capital theory and contemporary school reform, citations listed above and at the end of Chapter 8 contain a more than adequate coverage of most of these perspectives. My favorites from among the "conflict" texts are the works by Randall Collins and Aronowitz and Giroux. I have also used for classroom purposes *Youth: Transition to Adulthood* by James Coleman. This book presents a contemporary debate over the social puposes of schooling as distinguished from solely economic ones, even among "mainstream" perspectives (see Chapter 4).

In addition, there are a growing number of "interpretivist" texts and studies currently available that I have not discussed. *Learning to Labor* (New York: Columbia University Press, 1977) has already become a classic in this tradition. Other representative works in this emerging area that I have found interesting include Henry Giroux's *Ideology, Culture, and the Process of Schooling* (Philadelphia: Temple University Press, 1981); Jay MacLeod's *Ain't No Makin' It* (Boulder, CO: Westview Press, 1987); and *Between Two Worlds: Black Students in an Urban Community College* (Boston: Routledge & Kegan Paul, 1985), by Lois Weis.

CHAPTER 10

Education for Economic Development: Can We Transcend the Conventional Wisdom?

During the past two hundred years, ever-increasing economic growth has been eloquently posited as the solution for most of the social and economic problems of the world by a variety of economists, political economists, and social scientists. Proponents of this view, from Adam Smith onward, have claimed that unrestricted (and, more recently, government-assisted) growth in the private sector can and will improve the material well-being of all citizens, end poverty, and provide opportunities for individual moral and intellectual improvement. This text has briefly outlined the unfolding of this logic, paying particular attention to how successfully various social scientists and leaders in both the private and public sector have functioned in attempting to "reform" schools for economic development purposes.

At various times during our history, moral, political, and intellectual issues were the center-stage concerns of schooling. Yet, because of beliefs that educational innovation ought to be systematically linked to both economic development and social progress, many early concerns of educators were either swept away or have become second-order priorities in various waves of late nineteenth- and twentieth-century school reform.

Morality concerns of schools and churches in the eighteenth and early nineteenth century (before industrialization) became incorporated into public education in the form of character training. While such training was indeed related to earlier interests in preparing "morally upright" individuals (as defined by Protestant standards), its specific focus by the late nineteenth century was to help prepare students for entry into an emerging capitalist work world. Here, it was argued, good moral habits were seen as prerequisites to good business and good worker habits.

Similarly, early and mid-nineteenth-century concerns over democratic participation and political leadership have also become less explicitly addressed academic ideals of American public school educators during the past hundred years. According to emerging interpretations of social scientists, economic development was (and is) systematically related to social progress (and more recently, modernization). Under this view, rational decision making and efficiency concerns of the private sector inevitably bring about advances in human social relations. Given this perspective, the role of the school has become one of extending the process of economic development not only for the sake of economic productivity and the improvement of individual standards of living, but also because such development is believed to bring about positive social change.

School reforms in twentieth-century America, then, have continually deemphasized specific inquiry and debate regarding such topics as democracy, morality, and inequality. Instead, school reformers and much of the public have come to believe that continuing the thrust of economic development by better adjusting the process of schooling to the needs of the private sector ought to be the central issue in "improving" public education. The sociologists Francisco Ramirez and John Boli-Bennett have further argued that formal education is seen not only in America but also around the world today as *the* central link between individual opportunities and national development. Thus, educational programming and school reforms around the globe have now come to be ideologically equated with advances in economic and social improvement.[1] (See Table 10.1.)

In the United States, the most recent wave of school reform continues to target the role schools "ought" to take in regard to enhancing economic development at the end of the twentieth century. Beginning in 1983, school reform reports issued by various private organizations and civic groups argue that schools can be of even greater use to U.S. economic productivity once they begin to re-emphasize academic excellence (particularly in science and math). Borrowing from contemporary human capital theory, advocates of using the school to better prepare our "human resources" (i.e., children) declare that more specific attention needs to be given to the "productive" rather than "consumptive" possibilities of schooling. By making our schools more rigorous, it is argued, we will enhance both our national economy and the material and social lives of our children. This will occur because more productive workers mean a more productive economy, and a more productive economy means a higher standard of living for all our citizens.

TABLE 10.1. ESTIMATED POPULATION, SCHOOL ENROLLMENT, TEACHERS, AND PUBLIC EXPENDITURES FOR EDUCATION IN MAJOR AREAS OF THE WORLD: 1970–71, 1980–81, AND 1983–84

Item	World Total[1]	Africa	Asia[2]	Europe[3]	Central and South America[4]	Northern America[4]	Oceania[5]
1	*2*	*3*	*4*	*5*	*6*	*7*	*8*
Population, all ages,[6] in thousands	3,683,455	357,311	2,095,362	701,125	283,763	226,565	19,330
Enrollment, all levels,[7] in thousands	37,708	2,438	18,745	8,855	3,754	3,647	268
First (primary) level	19,929	1,714	10,740	3,593	2,245	1,510	126
Second level[8]	14,149	632	6,967	4,100	1,114	1,225	112
Third level[9]	3,631	93	1,038	1,162	396	912	30
Teachers, all levels,[7] in thousands	39,757	2,992	19,806	8,986	4,118	3,580	276
First (primary) level	21,007	2,050	11,382	3,609	2,379	1,466	122
Second level[8]	14,765	819	7,232	4,158	1,273	1,161	123
Third level[9]	3,984	123	1,192	1,220	466	952	31
Public expenditures on education, in millions of U.S. dollars	$628,528	$16,634	$114,204	$211,727	$26,513	$248,595	$10,856
As a percent of gross national product	5.7	5.3	4.6	5.5	4.0	6.9	5.9
1980–81							
Population, all ages,[10] in thousands	4,453,155	475,983	2,590,697	749,431	362,130	251,885	23,030
Enrollment, all levels,[7] in thousands	847,634	79,566	477,675	138,962	87,145	59,510	4,776
First (primary) level	558,465	63,256	330,607	67,455	64,804	29,640	1,704
Second level[8]	241,984	14,941	133,240	57,752	17,511	16,885	1,655
Third level[9]	47,185	1,368	13,828	13,756	4,830	12,986	417
Teachers, all levels,[7] in thousands	37,708	2,438	18,745	8,855	3,754	3,647	268
First (primary) level	19,929	1,714	10,740	3,593	2,245	1,510	126
Second level[8]	14,149	632	6,967	4,100	1,114	1,225	112
Third level[9]	3,631	93	1,038	1,162	396	912	30
Public expenditures on education, in millions of U.S. dollars	$612,573	$16,714	$101,589	$250,753	$32,898	$220,231	$10,388
As a percent of gross national product	5.6	4.8	4.5	5.6	4.0	7.0	5.9

1983–84							
Population, all ages,[11] in thousands	4,842,048	553,210	2,824,008	770,382	406,223	263,404	24,820
Enrollment, all levels,[7] in thousands	873,795	92,338	485,547	138,238	93,700	59,108	4,864
First (primary) level	572,140	71,319	334,325	66,432	67,981	29,458	2,625
Second level[8]	250,143	19,339	135,186	57,475	20,229	16,129	1,786
Third level[9]	51,513	1,680	16,037	14,331	5,490	13,522	452
Teachers, all levels,[7] in thousands	39,757	2,992	19,806	8,986	4,118	3,580	276
First (primary) level	21,007	2,050	11,382	3,609	2,379	1,466	122
Second level[8]	14,765	819	7,232	4,158	1,273	1,161	123
Third level[9]	3,984	123	1,192	1,220	466	952	31
Public expenditures on education, in millions of U.S. dollars	$628,528	$16,634	$114,204	$211,727	$26,513	$248,595	$10,856
As a percent of gross national product	5.7	5.3	4.6	5.5	4.0	6.9	5.9

[1] Enrollment and teacher data exclude the Democratic People's Republic of Korea. Expenditure data exclude China and the Democratic People's Republic of Korea.

[2] Excludes the U.S.S.R., but includes both the Asian and the European portions of Turkey.

[3] Includes the U.S.S.R., but excludes the European portions of Turkey.

[4] Northern America includes Bermuda, Canada, Greenland, St. Pierre and Miquelon, and the United States of America. Hawaii is included in North America, not Oceania. Central and South America includes the rest of America.

[5] Includes American Samoa, Australia, Guam, and New Zealand.

[6] Data are for midyear 1970.

[7] Excludes preprimary, special, and adult education.

[8] General, teacher training, and other second level education of a vocational and technical nature.

[9] Universities and other institutions of higher education.

[10] Data are for midyear 1980.

[11] Data are estimated for 1985.

NOTE: Because of rounding, details may not add to totals. (Sources: United Nations Educational, Scientific, and Cultural Organization, Paris, Statistical Yearbook, 1985. [This table was prepared September 1986.])

HISTORICAL AND CONTEMPORARY ARGUMENTS AGAINST CAPITALIST DEVELOPMENT

As this text has attempted to show, the current conventional wisdom in America is that increasing economic development is possible, is desirable, and is a precursor to social progress. This ideology of economic development and social progress has increasingly dictated pedagogical and curricular reforms in American education. Regardless of the objective inaccuracies or weaknesses in these ideological beliefs, it seems quite likely that the equating of economic development with social progress and the linking of schooling objectives with economic development will intensify in the future, rather than the reverse.

Yet, significant criticisms of these movements are also quite apparent in the literature of economics and the social sciences for those who care to study them. Many early and contemporary criticisms of the logic underlying limitless economic development and the role the school might have in its unfolding are detailed in several chapters of this book. And while there is no room in this chapter to review all that has already been discussed, a paragraph or two "highlighting" some of these earlier opposing positions seems appropriate.

For example, contrary to arguments that capitalist economic development leads to social progress and the improvement of everyone's standard of living, we have reviewed arguments suggesting that the economic "payoff" for individuals from different social classes and ethnic groups is likewise quite varied. Indeed, contrary to suggestions that capitalists and entrepreneurs are to be admired and appreciated for their contribution to everyone's standard of living, there are those who lament the frivolity and irrationality of the capitalist system in creating demand for unnecessary products as opposed to meeting real human needs. And contrary to belief that our economic system leads to social progress, that it ought to provide a model for the rest of the world to emulate, and that public schools can help pave the way for economic development, we have reviewed a host of arguments disputing the notion that economic development continues to bring about progress, that other countries can use our model to improve their economic status, or that education ought to be in the economic development business at all.

Furthermore, many critics of capitalism have noted the "unadvertised" features of capitalist economic development that they have found problematic. Early perspectives of writers like Robert Owen, for example, suggested that the loss of community under the promise of economic opportunity was too high a price to pay for unrestrained economic development. As career (geographic) mobility patterns now verify, and as human capital theory now explicitly calls for, stable and meaningful community life in the industrial world is a vanishing phenomenon. Instead, we talk of national communities and world communities linked by telecommunications, rather than by face to face interactions. In other words, the very concept of community (and the role schooling might have in enhancing it) is completely different near the end of the twentieth century from what it was prior to the Industrial Revolution.

In other parts of the world as well, many have come to criticize the ability of increased economic productivity to alleviate poverty and inequality on a planet already dominated by several powerful economies. While many Americans in both the private and public sectors acknowledge and look forward to increased business "opportunities" in the world economy, others fear for the fate of many less developed nations now the target of our economic development interests. In addition to the several Marxist versions of this perspective previously reviewed, even less ideologically committed sociologists like Peter Berger have argued against the possibility of contemporary capitalist economic and social theory for improving the economic quality of life of many people in less developed nations:

> The capitalist ideology of development is geared to the growth of an economy which, at least in its essential character, is based on the market. The critique of this ideology has two fundamental questions: Who benefits? and Who decides? The questions can also be put as Whose growth? and Whose market? . . . The ideology of development has long maintained that the benefits will eventually extend to all sectors of society. This tenet has been called the "trickle-down effect," more optimistically the "spread effect." . . . [however, critics] have been able to show that the evidence on the Third World to date gives little support to the pious hopes of the "spread effect." In much of the Third World there has been an *increasingly* polarized distribution in income and wealth. That is, the lower classes have been getting *less,* not more, as the process unfolds. Nor has their absolute conditon improved appreciably, if at all. There is *more* hunger and *more* disease today than there was some decades ago, not just in terms of absolute figures but even when the increase in population is taken into account. What is more, in much of the Third World there has been an increase in unemployment and underemployment.[2]

ARE THERE LIMITS TO ECONOMIC DEVELOPMENT?

As the preceding paragraphs suggest, there are various well-rehearsed criticisms of the utility of economic development theory for enhancing the social lives of all Americans and people in other countries. So too, a variety of economists and social critics have emerged over the past several decades who suggest new weaknesses in our economic development theories,

theories that they point out had their origin hundreds of years ago. Since these more modern criticisms have appeared in the popular press, they are undoubtedly not new to you.

Some observers suggest that political and economic confrontations between capitalist nations and/or between capitalist and socialist ones must eventually lead (again) to war. One commonplace argument, for example, suggests that the continual escalation of competition for scarce resources and consumer markets for products must continually lead to armed confrontation between nation-states. In a nuclear age, such confrontations could spell the end for the entire human race.

There are those who have been eloquent in castigating the *inefficiencies* of economic development in industrialized nations, like the British economist E.F. Schumacher. In his widely read book, *Small Is Beautiful,* Schumacher argued that the planet's resources were finite, and that far too many of these resources were being consumed by inhabitants of the already developed nations. The ideology of unlimited economic development, he argued, is based on faulty assumptions about the level of exploitation the planet can sustain. According to Schumacher:

> Modern man does not experience himself as a part of nature but as an outside force destined to dominate and conquer it. He even talks of a battle with nature, forgetting that, if he won the battle, he would find himself on the losing side. . . . The illusion of unlimited powers, nourished by astonishing scientific and technological achievements, has produced the concurrent illusion of having solved the problem of production. The latter illusion is based on the failure to distinguish between income and capital where the distinction matters most. Every economist and businessman is familiar with the distinction, and applies it conscientiously and with considerable subtlety to all economic affairs—except where it really matters: namely, the irreplaceable capital which man has not made, but simply found, and without which he can do nothing.[3]

Following upon arguments like Schumacher's, many contemporary environmental groups point out that unlimited economic development schemes of the nineteenth and twentieth century have failed to consider the natural limitations that the air, water, and soil resources of the planet place on economic growth, and they typically suggest that our population problems are far from solved after hundreds of years of economic growth.[4] Significantly, the ranks of many of these environmental groups are also filled with economists. Yet, while economists who believe in the possibility and practicality of zero-growth and/or ecologically sustainable economic development are easy to find, their conspicuous absence from U.S. economic development advisory panels and school reform groups continues to demonstrate the ideological bias of our culture toward a system that these economists claim cannot work.

Such critics therefore take issue not only with the dominant ideology of economic growth, but with educational philosophies that encourage continued exploitation of the planet's resources for economic gain (see Box 10.1). A self-proclaimed critic of unlimited expansion of economic development, Jeremy Rifkin, urged a completely different ethical and practical stance with regard to future notions about such growth:

> The most important truth about ourselves, our artifacts and our civilization is that it is all borrowed. . . . We are forever borrowing from the environment to create and maintain the totality of our way of life. We borrow resources from nature and transform them into utilities in order to gain some temporary measure of economic well-being. . . . The moment we introduce the idea of borrowing into economics a sense of responsibility suddenly enters the picture, because with borrowing comes the notion of indebtedness. . . . Implicit in the concept of borrowing and debt is the idea of paying back. Borrowing, then, has built-in limits. One should borrow only to the extent that one can pay back. A civilization should borrow only to the extent it can pay back.[5]

Furthermore, argues Rifkin, an educational philosophy that operates in the name of environmental concerns is also one that may ensure the survival of the human race. For, as he suggests, international acquisitiveness (i.e., the struggle for shares of the international marketplace) underlies the ever-present potential for nuclear war. As he puts it:

> There is much talk today in big and small places about saving the world from extinction by redirecting the affairs of nations. But if we are even to hope to do that, we must also talk about saving the human mind by redirecting the individual and collective consciousness of the human race.
>
> . . . The politics of a civilization are largely determined by the way it chooses to pursue knowledge, the way it chooses to use tools and the way it chooses to organize its economic activity. . . . Therefore, if we are to redefine the concept of security, we need to rethink our basic assumptions about the pursuit of knowledge, our relationship to technology, and the nature of the economic process.[6]

WHAT OUGHT TO BE THE FOCUS OF AMERICAN SCHOOLING?

I have argued that convictions about education and its purpose are primarily influenced by economic and social concerns of powerful groups external to the school. Yet, most citizens of our nation, not just powerful individuals in the private sector, now believe in the ideology of economic development and

---

BOX 10.1   Has Economic Development Solved the Overpopulation Problem?

World Population Could Double in Next 40 Years

By Randolph Schmid (Associated Press)

WASHINGTON—By the time they reach middle age, Americans born today could be sharing the planet with twice the current number of people, a private population research group reported yesterday.

The world's population, which edged past the 5 billion mark just a year ago, could double within 40 years, the Population Reference Bureau said in its annual "World Population Data Sheet."

"We've been noticing for a couple of years now that the overall growth trend has not been following the standard projections," Carl Haub, an analyst for the bureau, said in a telephone interview.

The expected decline in birth rates in many less-developed nations has not been as great as hoped, he said, and "it is likely that the sixth billion (person) will be added in just 10 more years."

While projecting the world's population requires assumptions about birth rates, Haub said that the global population had been increasing faster than previously expected.

There is a perception that world population growth is a problem of the 1970s, Haub observed, "so we thought it was time to point out that it's still growing faster than had been projected."

The bureau's data sheet shows worldwide population growing at 1.7 percent annually. The United Nations had projected growth of 1.6 percent.

"That doesn't sound like much," Haub said, but in a world of 5 billion inhabitants, the difference represents 5 million more people each year.

Population growth has not followed the smooth trend downward that had been expected in many developing nations, Haub said.

The doubling of the world population in 40 years depends on growth continuing at 1.7 percent, but population growth rates for individual countries vary, Haub said.

The more developed nations, for example, are growing at 0.6 percent annually, for an expected doubling time of 120 years, the data sheet shows. On the other hand, the less-developed nations could double in just 33 years, at a growth rate of 2.1 percent.

(Reprinted from the Lexington Herald Leader, *April 28, 1988, with the permission of the Associated Press.)*

---

growth. As capitalism in America has "matured," so too have schooling objectives and priorities increasingly become focused on perceived needs of the private sector, broadly defined.

The conventional wisdom in the United States today, therefore, is that improved academic performance by our students and more years of schooling completed will bring about continued economic development and social progress. Yet, while this is the conventional wisdom, and while it seems logical to assume that better trained individuals do better work and improve the productive process, the scientific understanding of how all of this works is methodologically incomplete and the subject of much debate. Importantly, many highly respected economists and sociologists have taken positions in opposition to "supply-side" human capital formation arguments, particularly as this overly simplistic view has been relied upon by many school reformers of the late twentieth century.

Yet, competing facts and alternative theoretical formations have a strange way of being ignored when they stand in the way of ideology. My feeling is that facts and theories opposed to current human capital notions will probably matter little either to leaders in private industry, who continually seek ways to transfer occupational training costs to the public sector, or to civic leaders attempting to attract industry based on calculated inventories of the occupational skills of their local, state, or national human resources. The analysis pursued throughout this text suggests that our schools will continue to be the target of private and public sector pressure to better conform schooling outcomes with perceived technological needs of our post-industrial economy. Even though the actual skills required for this society are in dispute, "investment decisions" by students from different class and ethnic backgrounds have been too little considered (see Box 10.2).

Paradoxically, perhaps, many of my own notions about the "proper" objectives of public schooling were first championed by some of the political economists who typically did not foresee the ideologically constraining possibilities of the economic system they believed would liberate human life. Many of my own views are also consistent with later critics of schooling for economic growth purposes. I believe, for example, that schools *should* teach children how to read and how to "do" mathematics. Yet, I believe that the teaching of such subjects ought to be accomplished within substantive curricula and not primarily in a skill-based regimen. I also believe that issues of political governance and democracy ought to be central in any school curriculum. Given the political apathy of citizens in this country (as evidenced by low voter turnout for almost any election, and the lack of political debate over topics like the ones discussed in this text), such curricular concerns appear to require serious attention.

Moral and ethical issues likewise would occupy an important place in any curriculum I would outline, were I asked to propose one. While there can be no denying that many residents of Western nations enjoy a material standard of living never believed possible by our ancestors, this rapid advance in material standard of living has not been matched by equally rapid improvements in the quality of our social life. In other words, social progress and modernization trends seen to date in this country have not by themselves demonstrated to me an ability to improve our values and ideals

---

**BOX 10.2   Alternative Versions of School Reform
Sponsored by Prominent Educators**

*Saying Reforms Fail Most Pupils, Shanker Argues for a "New Type"
of Teaching Unit*

By Lynn Olson

WASHINGTON—Arguing that most education-reform measures are resulting in "more of the same," the president of the American Federation of Teachers last week outlined a plan that would enable small groups of teachers and parents to create their own innovative schools within existing school buildings.

Such a step is needed, the union leader, Albert Shanker, asserted in a speech before the National Press Club here, because the reform movement is "bypassing about 80 percent of the students in this country."

"Eighty percent of students do not learn in traditional settings," he contended. "They just don't fit."

Mr. Shanker disputed Secretary of Education William J. Bennett's contention that the reform movement has been "highjacked and held for ransom" by education bureaucrats and special-interest groups.

In fact, the A.F.T. president asserted, the "top down" approach to school reform—typified by state legislation and mandates—"is the most widely implemented set of reforms within my memory."

The problem, he said, is that "there is not one shred of evidence that they work for more than about 10 to 20 percent of our students." Simply requiring students to meet more and higher standards, Mr.Shanker argued, "will not do anything for those students who are not able to sit still and listen, who are not able to read on their own" and who, when asked a question, "are humiliated in front of all of their colleagues in class, because they never get it right."

(*Reprinted with permission from* Education Week, *April 6, 1988.*)

---

without specific discussion, understanding, and debate. While most schools do deal with aspects of moral life within their curricula, and while some of the currently popular school reform reports briefly mention this concern, attention to moral and ethical questions needs to again become a prominent concern of schooling, not one relegated to second-order significance. It might even be time to bring god back into the American classroom, if only to help underscore the fact that once upon a time questions of beliefs and values preceded talk of economic development, rather than the reverse. Of course, the study of religious beliefs and values in my curriculum would most likely follow a comparative perspective, where the focus would be on the different religious systems and their typically unique answers to important moral questions.

There are already many today who suggest that the subject of "understanding our economic system" needs to occupy more space in the secondary school curriculum. I agree; however, the study of economic systems in my curriculum would go far beyond such ideologically convenient topics as "exploring the dynamics of the free market system" or "learning how the stock market works." Rather, since my belief is that economic systems and economic development significantly influence all other social dynamics and greatly affect notions about "appropriate social behavior" and "healthy personality formation," courses that I would develop for public education would focus on these themes. Within such courses we would examine the meaning and purpose of human communities in different sorts of economic systems and find out what happens to them under different types of economic change. We would also talk about the possibility and desirability of economic growth within various economic models and with regard to different environmental conditions. And much of all this discussion would focus on non-Western economic notions and systems as well as on those apparent among Western nations today.

SUGGESTIONS ON HOW TO RESIST
THE CONVENTIONAL WISDOM

The preceding abbreviated list of school reforms I would like to see accomplished in public education is indeed a parsimonious one. Contrary to many of my more liberal colleagues, I hold out little hope that the logic of education for economic development in this country will yield significantly to my vision of what schools ought to look like or what they ought to teach. Rather than focusing on the construction of alternative educational models and the crusade for their adoption, my own academic interests have focused on debunking the "logic" of typically illogical or quasi-logical social processes; I leave it to others to construct the models or processes I might favor. Among the current educational theories there are several I admire, and there are others easy to debunk (frequently they are one and the same).

The current conventional wisdom in America today, which argues that more schooling leads to more productivity which leads to improved standards of living for all, is in my judgment a quasi-logical theory for "improving" American education. This does not mean, in my opinion, that our schools need no reform. Many of our schools, particularly those "serving" the already disadvantaged, need serious attention.[7] Yet, even raising the academic performance levels of students from lower social backgrounds will not, in my opinion, significantly improve their chances of employment in the future, nor their ability to contribute to the further economic productivity of our nation. Rather, improving educational outcomes for such individuals may merely enable them to remain occupationally in about the same situation as their parents, at the bottom of a segmented labor system. Most "disadvantaged" students need to be better educated just to survive in our economic system. Yet, such survival does not guarantee any upward social mobility (see Box 10.3).

Instead (again, in my opinion) it is the structure of opportunities that needs serious attention in this country, not just the entry level skills of our future workers. If our workplace were to become "democraticized," and if the manual as well as the organizational skills of our young adults were more fully utilized in the productive process, we would have a more productive economy. Because many of the skills acquired in school (and on the job) go unrecognized and underutilized in the private sector, the quest for better jobs (e.g., those actually allowing for more control over various aspects of work) forces many Americans to return to school for more credentials. Such a fact certainly helps colleges to expand and grow and apparently increases correlations between years of schooling and productivity. Yet, for many jobs, this is probably a spurious relationship.

Of course, this is not to suggest that educational opportunities in America ought to be restricted or that colleges ought to be shut down. Rather, I would argue that educational opportunities ought to be increased and extended for both "productive" as well as "consumptive" purposes. Adults in the future will need to be retrained; economically successful citizens of the nation would seek out and benefit from community education courses, college offerings, and other post-secondary opportunities. To be a truly education-minded culture we should discard the notion that education is primarily for children and adolescents, or that education is synonymous with years of schooling attended, scores on standardized tests, or credentials acquired.

However, while such possibilities may occur someday, the only way to compete with today's conventional wisdom is both to point out the scientific weaknesses of this "wisdom" and to reemphasize competing notions about

---

BOX 10.3   Should We Rethink Where to Invest Our Educational Dollars?

"Self-Interest and the Common Weal": Focusing on the Bottom Half

By M. Sandra Reeves

Whenever America gets serious about an issue, it reaches for the right metaphor, for language that will simplify and give power to ideas. Thus, it was not by accident that the report of the National Commission on Excellence in Education—issued five years ago this week—sounded more at times like a replay of World War II than a prelude to school reform.

Even the document's title, *A Nation At Risk,* was a call to arms. And its rhetoric, heavy on economic and achievement comparisons with former enemies, principally Japan, sustained the alarm.

"If an unfriendly power had attempted to impose on America the mediocre educational performance that exists today," it read, "we might have viewed it as an act of war. . . . We have, in effect, been committing an act of unthinking, unilateral educational disarmament."

What is ironic, on this fifth anniversary of its release is not that *A Nation At Risk* failed to instill its sense of urgency—virtually every state has acted to impose its recommended higher standards—but that a message implicit in its international comparisons has been, until recently, all but ignored.

The Japanese achieve their extremely high *average* level of academic performance by taking great care to see that their weakest students do well. As they have often claimed, they have "the best bottom 50 percent in the world" educationally—and virtually no dropouts.

American school reform, on the other hand, was launched with a rhetoric of "excellence" that did not take into account the bottom 50 percent.

It is an omission that many have seized upon in assessing the movement's progress at the half-decade mark.

In a report on urban education released last month, the trustees of the Carnegie Foundation for the Advancement of Teaching note a "disturbing gap between reform rhetoric and results."

"We are deeply troubled," they say, "that a reform movement launched to upgrade *all* students is irrelevant to many children—largely black and Hispanic—in our urban schools."

Albert Shanker, president of the American Federation of Teachers, wrote in a recent newspaper column that "what now mostly passes for reform has been an especially empty gesture when it comes to our most disadvantaged students and schools."

A William T. Grant Foundation study released this year warns that though some reforms are promising, "a sizeable number of youth—too many for a pragmatic or a just society to ignore—already suffer the consequences of school failure."

And in a new publication from the National Education Association, the Harvard University economist Robert B. Reich says, when assessing the future needs of the U.S. workforce, that "we will have to do a better job . . . helping all our children become minimally numerate and literate."

The attention, it would seem, is turning more and more to what the authors of a new Ford Foundation study, *Toward a More Perfect Union,* call "the second achievement gap."

This gap is a domestic one, they say, "one between the bottom scorers and the top scorers, between minorities and nonminorities, and between the poor and the nonpoor."

What—or Who—Is in Jeopardy?

The locus of America's "risk" is shifting from the nation as a whole to its children. And, as it does, a variant of the excellence commission's rhetoric is becoming the most widely used term in the educational lexicon: "students at risk."

(Reprinted with permission from Education Week, *April 27, 1988.)*

how education and economic development might be linked. What can contemporary economics of education studies really tell us about educational policy? Not as much as many would like to think. Economists tend to agree that basic literacy is important for economic development, that workers seem to learn important occupational skills related to increased productivity, and that under ideal conditions workers are interested in investing in training programs that would improve their employment possibilities and those of their children. Given such "facts" we might just as well concentrate most of our public monies on early childhood and elementary education. Similarly, we might allow students to leave school earlier instead of later, in order to place them in occupational training programs leading to good jobs, not just those demanding low-level skills. We might provide a host of institutional settings where adult learners could return to school for new skills related to new careers. There are other policies we might pursue based on the economics of education, but they would probably be even further divorced from empirical justification than those I have just mentioned.

As this very brief list suggests, I believe that problems of production in our economy do demand the attention of the public schools. However, they demand very different policies from those called for by many contemporary school reformers. At the same time, my list of curricular objectives for public education suggests many other (and in my opinion even more central) concerns for schools than those that can be defended on purely economic development grounds.

In good liberal fashion, then, I seem to be in agreement with many of the early political economists and some later critics of the dynamics of American capitalism. The purpose of our economic system ought to be to help satisfy the material and social conditions of human life, not the reverse. If problems of production within our economic system lead to redefining children primarily as "human resources" for economic development purposes, we have more than problems of production; we have problems of interpretation, values, and priorities. Redesigning the economic system, rather than redefining its resources, seems to me the more logical course of action. And resisting the rationale and programs designed to even further link misguided notions about the purpose of economic growth and development ought to be encouraged in our schools.

NOTES

1. Francisco Ramirez and John Boli-Bennett, "Global Patterns of Educational Institutionalization," in Philip Altbach, Robert Arnove and Gail Kelley (eds.), *Comparative Education*. New York: Macmillan, 1982, pp. 15–36.

2. Peter Berger, *Pyramids of Sacrifice: Political Ethics and Social Change*. New York: Basic Books, 1974, pp. 46–47.
3. E. F. Schumacher, *Small is Beautiful: Economics as if People Mattered*. New York: Harper and Row, 1973, p. 14.
4. See, for example, Lester R. Brown et al., *The State of the World 1988: A Worldwatch Institute Report on Progress Toward a Sustainable Society*. New York: Norton, 1988.
5. Jeremy Rifkin, *Declaration of a Heretic*. Boston: Routledge & Kegan Paul, 1985, p. 97.
6. *Ibid.*, p. 82.
7. Henry Levin, "The Educationally Disadvantaged: A National Crisis." Working Paper #6, The State Youth Initiatives Project. Philadelphia, PA. Public/Private Ventures, July, 1985.

FOR ADDITIONAL READING

In addition to the works listed above and the related books mentioned in Chapter 9, the themes outlined in this chapter are also related to much of the (even more liberal) focus of Edward Stevens and George Wood in *Justice, Ideology, and Education* (New York: Random House, 1987) and of Barbara Presseisen's *Unlearned Lessons: Current and Past Reforms for School Improvement* (Philadelphia: Falmer Press, 1985).

Index

Page numbers in italics refer to tables and boxed items.

181